Dear World, See What I See

My Vegan Path

SHANTI URRETA

Vegan Publishers™

Published by:
Vegan Publishers, Danvers, MA, www.veganpublishers.com

Cover and text design: Nicola May Design
Cover Photo: Carlos Urreta

♻ Printed in the United States of America on 100% recycled paper

ISBN 978-1-940184-15-9

Table of Contents

Reviews and Letters

"The ultimate truth will often go through phases of ridicule, opposition, and, finally, general acceptance. In order for general acceptance to occur with anything, it is necessary for visionaries to drive that message. Shanti Urreta has sought the ultimate truth with regards to embracing a plant-based diet and is sharing it with all in this relaxed and informal book. Her mission and responsibility is to empower someone to take a second look at our diet as a nation and our cruel practices that are performed on animals for the sake of enjoying a meal. Furthermore, the book highlights the environmental downside of these large farming practices and the options or pathways people can embrace in creating a new setting where all organisms will thrive.

Shanti Urreta has that vision, passion, drive, and, yes, responsibility to open people's eyes and develop compassion to all animals on this planet. She writes about it in a way that truly envelops compassion to all animals. The karmic references will raise the eyebrows of even the most hardened and isolated of individuals with regards to a plant-based diet.

Shanti delightfully explains the benefits of eating a plant-based diet for your overall health and admonishes the traditional meat, dairy, and sugar diets that are a part of our culture. Plus, she rebukes the notion that a plant-based diet is a boring diet. In fact, I can wholeheartedly say it is both delicious and nutritious, something we can all benefit from!"

—Dr. William Brightman, MS, the chiropractor who steered Shanti toward a plant-based diet; an educator, family man, and an honest, humble, caring human being

"I am so busy that I decided to just glance at the book. But, I ended up putting everything aside to keep reading the book because it grabbed me. It touched my heart and curiosity from the first pages. It is so down to earth and genuine. Feels like you are talking intimately with the reader....including me. Love this. So glad this will be out in the world."

—Rae Sikora, author of *Plant Peace Daily* and co-founder of The Institute for Humane Education, VegFund, and Plant Peace Daily; a very special person to all who know her

"I read *See What I See*, the first time for enjoyment and that happened. More importantly, however, I gleaned a sense of urgency, for my own life force, based on what my body has been telling me, and what I had suspected all along, but in spite of, perhaps because of the questions I was asking, I could never seem to get the answers I was seeking. I am assuming I was either asking the wrong questions or asking the wrong people. Suddenly, as I read your book there was a spark, a moment of connection, of revelation, of explanation, and I knew instinctively what my next steps were. Just as when I stopped smoking so many years ago, this transition is going to be 'cold turkey' (no pun intended). All of the physical ailments I have been experiencing can be traced directly to my diet. Answer? Simple! Your book was key to the change I needed. The only question that remains is will the change happen in time?

All I have is the here and now. The past is history, and there is no guarantee of a tomorrow, so all I have is today, and yesterday is when my awareness began, but the real beginning was when I met you. I knew in that moment we shared together that there was something powerful about you that I did not fully understand, but had to learn about. I have not regretted a single second of my new path of discovery. For that, I am grateful, to you and *See What I See*."

—Bruce Grecke, a 70-year-old Home Depot employee

and a talented writer who befriended Shanti and "carried"
her along as she worked to finish the first edition of this book

Dedication

To all of humanity and especially to all the "Christines," who, once they know, must do.

For the animals.

Letter to the Reader

"We are ethical if we abandon our stubbornness, if we surrender our strangeness toward other creatures and share in the life and the suffering that surround us. Only this quality makes us truly human."[1]
—Albert Schweitzer

Dear World,

I have written this book to you from my heart. Thank you for reading it. I feel honored and grateful.

This book is a transcendental story told very simply. It is a story not common to the human experience, a result of my being on a path that is the least traveled. This experience, although with different stories, is shared by only 2–3 percent of the United States population.[2]

Please read this book from the beginning to end. It is important not to skip around. You will understand it better that way.

With deep gratitude,

Shanti

In This World Together

I consider myself to be an eclectic spiritual person—I take a little from here and a little from there. Whatever makes sense to me is what I consider to be my truth.

The other day I heard a story taken from the Zohar, the kabbalistic wisdom that explains the secrets of the Bible, the universe, and every aspect of life. It's about these two men on opposite sides of a boat. The first man begins to drill a hole on his side of the boat, and the second man says, "Hey, what are you doing? Why are you doing that?" And the first man replies, "What do you care? It is on my side of the boat, not yours."

We are all in this world together. What we do affects the whole. *Every decision* we make affects the whole. Our goal as a society is to become more aware of our decisions and *what* they affect so that we can do better.

The goal of this book is to raise that level of awareness.

Even if you have many things to do that are taking priority in your life, as most of us do these days, please make this book a priority along with the other important things. In order to be better, our level of awareness has to be increased. It will take a little bit of work—namely, to read this book and have conversations with others about the content, then see where life takes us.

* * *

Dreams can come true. I believe that. And so I dream.

This book asks for all of humanity to not only dream of the possibility that we can rid the world of violence and hatred, but also believe that peace is possible. In a message to the world in his book *The Philosophy of Civilization*, humanitarian and 1952 Nobel Peace Prize winner Albert Schweitzer (1875–1965) said, "Only such thinking as establishes the sway of the mental attitude of reverence for life can bring to mankind perpetual peace."[3] We have come to know those words as, "Until he extends his circle of compassion to all living beings, man himself will not find peace." Unfortunately, society was not ready for his message then. Perhaps we are ready now.

Most of us are very compassionate people—with our families, with our friends, and even with our cats and dogs. Karma says we should be living in a kind and compassionate world. Unfortunately, we know we are not.

This book takes a look at what we are doing, how without realizing it, we are promoting violence. We are putting violence out there from the food that we eat, from the clothes that we wear, from the science that we support, and from the entertainment that we choose. It only makes sense that violence will come back to us. And only when we see that connection, that karmic connection, can we begin to heal ourselves.

My story begins seven years ago with a life changing event: a trip to the doctor.

This book starts there and takes you on a journey—a journey that involves food, animals, the planet, and spirituality.

I dream that people will see what I saw on that journey, because after I saw the terror and the violence, I saw peace.

I dream that society is ready to hear Albert Schweitzer's message—that we are ready to extend our circle of compassion to all beings so that we, humankind, can finally have peace and give ourselves a better chance of survival as a species.

My Story

Dear World,

My name is Shanti. My parents gave me that name at birth. It means "peace."

I am half East Indian, half Puerto Rican. I am not fluent in Spanish but can understand a little bit, so I consider myself "Sorta Rican." I grew up in the Bronx eating rice and beans, pork chops, and "tostones" (fried plantains). I am married and have two children, ages twenty-five and twenty-nine. I was a teacher for twenty years in a small city with a mostly black and Hispanic population. I recently retired from the school system at the age of fifty-five. Until I was forty-seven, life was pretty much normal: I got married, had kids, bought a house in the country, and worked to pay the bills.

My story begins with going for a yearly physical at the age of forty-seven. The results came back showing slight anemia—low iron in my blood. The doctor sent me to a hematologist, a blood doctor. I figured it was no big deal. I would go and get a prescription for iron tablets, and everything would be fine. The waiting room had older patients waiting their turns. There were articles on the walls about people healed from cancer. I did not understand. I was uncomfortable being there. But I still figured I would just get the prescription for iron and be on my way.

The doctor called me into his office after waiting for what seemed like a really long time. He seemed rather uncomfortable, but I did not think anything of it. He then told me, rather nervously, that I had multiple myeloma. I had to ask him what that was, as I had never heard of it. And he told me, "Multiple myeloma is a blood cancer, and it will be a painful death as your bones begin to break."

I remember being in shock, like someone had just hit me with a bat. My mother was waiting for me in the waiting room. The last person I wanted to see at that moment was my mother. At eighty-two years old, she did not need to hear news like this. I remember sitting outside of the hospital on the curb, calling my husband on the phone, and crying.

I could not eat. I could not sleep. The little food that I did eat did not stay in my body for very long. My hands shook constantly, and I cried often. My whole family was pretty much in shock, just walking around, not really knowing how to be or what to say.

I looked on the Internet and read that a diagnosis of multiple myeloma meant that I had five years to live. How could this be happening? I had always dreamt that I would live to be a hundred years old, that I would be one of those little old ladies dancing on stage! What was happening?

At a following visit to the doctor, my husband and I were told the course of action: I would need to stay in the hospital for up to six weeks and have all of my blood taken out, cleaned, and put back in. Because of this, my immune system would be challenged, and I could easily get sick. That was the reason for the long hospital stay.

It was a strange time. Funny thing was that I felt fine. Things were happening very fast. It was a good thing my husband and I were teachers at the time and had the summer to deal with this.

And then a chiropractor friend of mine told me that I should stop eating meat and dairy, start buying organic fruits and vegetables, and begin juicing my vegetables in a juicer every day. I could fight this? I could heal my cancer? Multiple myeloma did not mean a death sentence?

This brought on more tough times. I did not know how to cook. I grew up in the fast food generation. We ate TV dinners, pizza, and potpies. I could no longer eat quick meals that I heated up in the oven. No more American cheese slices and Italian bread on the way home from work. No more stops to the pizza shop in town for a night out. No more baked chicken, my main meal. It all contained meat and dairy. On top of that, I had always thought that if a recipe had more than five ingredients in it, it was too much for me to handle, so cooking seemed daunting. But I had no choice. I had to figure it out or die soon. I had to learn how to eat for my life. I had to beat this cancer!

I bought books and started to read. It was tough for someone who was not really much of a reader, especially of those big books that I was trying to read. But I needed the information *immediately*. I could not wait till after I read these books to learn how to survive. I could not read fast enough! I had to start eating healthfully *that day*. But I did not know how.

I went through more blood tests, a painful bone marrow exam, and X-rays of every single bone. The doctors wanted to see how much damage, if any, had been done to the bones.

I needed to see how much work *I* had to do to survive.

Five weeks after the initial diagnosis, we took the results of the blood work, the bone marrow exam, and the X-rays, and went for a second opinion. Friends recommended that we go to another doctor who had come from Memorial Sloan Kettering Cancer Center in New York City. He was recommended as one of the best. We felt confident to go to him.

My husband and I sat across the desk from him as he flipped through the pages of my file, then looked up at us and said, "I don't see it." No bone damage? I held my breath, hoping to hear those words. And he said, "No, I don't see myeloma." The first diagnosis was wrong. The first doctor was wrong. He had read the results wrong.

And I wanted to hug the doctor, but instead I just started to cry. I was once again in shock. But now they were tears of joy.

* * *

Sometimes you come to a fork in the road of life, and you have to make a decision. "What school do I attend?" "Which house do we move to?" "Should I take that job or not?" They are conscious decisions that are left up to you to make.

But then sometimes life seems to grab you by the collar and drag you to a road that you have to be on, without you having any choice in it. It was like that. This was the road I was dragged to and forcibly put on.

After I had found out that it was a misdiagnosis, many people asked me if I sued the doctor. Did I go back to him? Did I let him have a piece of my mind? No, I didn't. I was not angry. I was so grateful to be alive—so grateful to not have cancer. I was so grateful for a second chance at life.

Life had just taken one amazing turn.

Living in gratitude,

Shanti

My Story Continues

Dear World,

I had decisions to make. I knew that life had changed for me. I knew I had been given something, but was not sure what it was. I just knew life was very different.

My chiropractor friend's words kept playing in my head: "Stop eating meat and dairy, buy organic fruits and vegetables, and juice your vegetables." It did not make sense to go back to eating the way I had before the diagnosis. I was told to get off of meat and dairy to cure my cancer. Why would I go back to eating it? Why wait to cure cancer if I could choose to prevent it?

I kept learning about food and what my body needed to stay healthy. I had to figure out what to eat and what to cook. One of the first things that made me question all of my past beliefs about food was a DVD called *Eating* by Mike Anderson. Joel Fuhrman, MD, author of *Eat to Live*, called it "A mind-blowing video experience that will forever change the way you think about food."[4] And change the way I think about food is just what it did.

I thought the *Eating* documentary was absolutely amazing. I was beginning to understand why I was eating a plant-based diet—why it was good for me, for my health. I loved beginning to understand how my body could not only survive on a plant-based diet, but also thrive!

I wanted to share this information with all of my friends. I wanted to share the health benefits. I wanted people to know that they could learn to *be* and *stay* healthy! I bought over thirty copies to lend out. I became obsessed with trying to share my newfound knowledge with everyone I met. This was such amazing information. Certain cancers could be cured? Diabetes could be reversed?

Heart disease could be prevented *and* reversed? Food could have an impact on arthritis, multiple sclerosis, Crohn's Disease, ear infections, allergies, acne, fibromyalgia, lupus, sexual functions, hot flashes, IBS, obesity, *multiple myeloma*, and so many of the diseases that we suffer from in the United States?[5]

I wanted to stand on a mountaintop and shout my new-found information to the world!

I thought everyone would want this information.

This was all happening at the same time my mother was suffering from heart disease. I gave her the DVD, but she would not watch it. She thought it was a gimmick, information that was silly. I tried to feed her the food that I was cooking, but she was more concerned about *me* getting the vitamins that I needed. She died two years later of heart failure after going through a few heart operations.

I continued to try to share this information with everyone I met. But person after person did not seem to care. They got angry with me because I became so persistent. I guess I became an "in your face" kind of person. I did not mean to get people angry. I just found this information so incredibly amazing. I wanted everyone to share in the goodness of it—the possibility of creating healthy lives for themselves! Why wouldn't they want it?

I even lent a DVD to someone who was in a position of power in my school district. She could have made a difference for our children, our teachers, and our parents. A real change could have been made for our small urban community. I was so excited at the idea of people in my school district learning how to be healthy. But the DVD was given back to me without a word. No conversation happened after that.

I went to my school district to see if there was anything I could do to make school food healthier. There wasn't. The district would have needed to hire a full-time employee just to try to make a difference. I got quiet. I stopped talking to the people who were in charge.

Parents of my students got angry with me for telling their children about a healthy diet, about the science of milk, and about my compassionate lifestyle. People in charge now had to talk to *me*!

I got even quieter. I stopped talking much to people at all. It is not easy to make and keep friends when the information that you have is so different from what most people are used to. It was hard for me to have conversations about Jennifer Lopez and the dress she wore at the music awards. I could not understand why people were talking about TV shows when there were so many more important conversations to be had.

I was frustrated. I had a hard time understanding why people did not care. My husband had a hard time understanding why I cared so much.

And then, while I hunted for information about food, I came upon sites that were "vegan." I found out that vegan was not just a way of eating but a way of living. I discovered sites that fought for the rights of animals, the animals that are killed for food. I began to see animals and appreciate them for what they are—beautiful beings. I saw *Earthlings*, a documentary narrated by Joaquin Phoenix, and became angry and sad, and I felt utterly disgusted and helpless about the reality of what we do to these beautiful beings in the name of food.

Yes, I had been given something. And now I knew what it was. I had been given a responsibility. A responsibility to speak— to speak for the animals, for justice, for compassion, for peace.

Peace,

Shanti

A Responsibility

Dear World,

A responsibility to speak. Yes, that is what I was given. And then life led me from one thing to the next, and years later I found myself with the need to write this book. I knew I had to speak. In school my lips were sealed about veganism. My job and my pension were at risk if I spoke about the fact that when we eat chicken, hamburgers, or bacon, we are actually eating animals. I was not allowed to speak about milk and how scientists say that milk can actually cause disease rather than do good for us.

I held back when our social studies curriculum said to teach about farms, "Then and Now." I knew I would have the principal knocking on my door if I shared the knowledge that I have of "now," and that was not something I wanted. No, I did not want to go down the same path as the teacher in New York City who was fired for speaking on behalf of the animals. So I was a "good girl" and hated every tight-lipped minute.

I always questioned living in a free-speech society. My husband tried to explain to me that I was a civil servant, that they pay me to teach what they tell me to teach. It was hard for me to understand. We were supposed to teach respect and kindness. I was trying to teach about compassion and kindness to all beings, but the school system that I was in did not allow me to do that.

I wanted to teach the children. I wanted their lives to be better than their parents' lives were. I wanted their world to be better than what their parents had. But I was not able to do that. My lips were sealed. So I retired from the school system—a system that I no longer totally believed in—and here I am. I left the public school system at the early age of fifty-five. I knew I had to do this; it was more important than staying at a well-paying job.

And it paid really well as teachers' salaries go. Making $124,000 a year is not something to give up easily in today's economy. But I did so because I felt the need to do something that my heart was telling me to do. Everything in life said it was time to choose something different than school. I did not know what was ahead of me. I just knew I had this urge to speak for the animals.

I imagined scenes like this: One day some second grade teacher will be reading a story with her students about the beautiful lion in the forest, the king of the jungle. And then she will tell the children how past civilizations killed them off and how we no longer have lions because they are extinct. And the teacher will be enraged because she knows that if enough people had cared, they could have done something. But not enough people cared.

I needed to be someone who cared.

* * *

So with the total support of my family, I left the teaching profession. And then life seemed to line up experiences that allowed me to get to the point where I knew I was going to write this book. I spoke to a most intriguing man, Dr. Anthony Gantt, a professional public speaker. He said to write a book if I wanted to become a speaker. I am truly grateful for his words.

I am driven to get a message to you in this book. A message from the grave of Albert Schweitzer. A message that needs to be heard:

by smart people and not-so-smart people
by rich people, poor people, and everyone in between
by kind and compassionate people
by young people who will one day be grown
by old people who will have spent their lives wondering
by the sad and the depressed
by the hopeless
by the curious

This is for all of you.

This message is also for those who are not so kind and caring—to those who steal, murder, and abuse, for the ones that find themselves in jail. Perhaps, just perhaps, it is not your fault that you are like you are. Life never seemed fair to you, and it probably wasn't. For some reason, you were the unlucky ones.

And in this book you will understand why that had to be so—why you, unfortunately, had to be the ones.

Just like you, there are some animals that are the "unlucky ones." Some animals are really lucky—the lap dogs, the dogs that sleep in beds, the cats and dogs that get clothes to wear during the holidays. And then there are the animals that are not so lucky. The ones that live their lives in cages, the ones that are tortured and killed.

It's those animals that we call our food, our entertainment, our clothes, and our science. Those, like you, are the unlucky ones.

And you certainly feel blamed for the ills of society. Some of you call yourselves "the bad ones." Perhaps we, "the fortunate ones," never took responsibility for our part in the way society is, for what life is like. Why should you take all the blame for how our streets are? Our communities? Our world?

This message is also for you.

This message is for all of humanity.

We are on this path of life together. We can either go one way or the other. At the end of one path is a world that is cruel and violent. And at the end of the other path is a world of kindness and compassion.

Albert Schweitzer spoke about extending our circle of compassion to include all living beings so that humankind can have peace.[6] It is our job to become conscious of *how* to extend that circle of compassion.

This was the responsibility I was given: to speak. To ask you if you are ready to hear a message of peace, to encourage you to become conscious of how to extend your circle of compassion so that humankind will have peace.

We look back at different times in history and wonder how people could have been so cruel: Hitler, times of slavery, wars, the slaughter of the Native Americans...I could go on and on. Do you ever think about how the everyday people just sat back and let these atrocities happen? How they did not stand up for the ones who were being abused? Wouldn't it be nice to be part of a society that stands up for the oppressed and says, "No more. We don't want these barbaric practices that we have in our lives to continue." And perhaps, just perhaps, mankind will finally have peace. Albert Schweitzer thought so.

Kind regards,

Shanti

The Food Journey

Dear World,

From a misdiagnosis seven years ago to speaking for animals and peace now—that is a long time with a lot of missing pieces in between.

So there I was. A person who had limited cooking skills trying to cook all my food. Not easy. And trying to feed a husband who did not like vegetables? Not easy at all! Fast forward seven years. I am eating steamed broccoli, sweet potato, lentil salad, and a zucchini patty as I write this. That's a long way from those days of Lean Cuisines and chicken sandwiches.

My husband, on the other hand, probably had an Amy's burrito and chips for lunch. He still cannot bring himself to eat vegetables without them being disguised. When I put broccoli in his "macaroni and cheez," it gets chopped finely so he does not have to taste chunks. He drinks green juices and smoothies made with kale, spinach, and other greens, so he gets some veggies. And he loves zucchini patties mixed with rice and beans. We have to trick him sometimes and not tell him that the food he is eating—and loving—has celery in it. (He really does not like celery. He is funny like that.)

The most important thing to me is that he eats a plant-based diet. He says he does it for his health, but I see him loving the animal rescues on television and showing his heart for the animals. He really is an animal lover. He grew up with a turtle walking around his house for years. He owned an alligator that he kept in a big tank and would sometimes put in the bathtub. He is intrigued by wildlife. He loves animals. I know he does.

For forty-seven years I had been eating a Standard American Diet. (It is called SAD for short, and with good reason, I have come to find.) Most Americans have also grown up with the SAD: burgers, fries, pizza, hot dogs, steaks, and dairy products.

My friend Christine has many friends whose lives revolve around food. They say half the fun of vacations is the food. For them, holiday traditions are built around food. Recipes are shared. Discussions are about food. Families get together with the traditional turkey for Thanksgiving, hot dogs and hamburgers for the Fourth of July, ham for Easter—and so on.

I did not grow up with steadfast traditions centered on food. We did have the turkey for Thanksgiving and "pasteles" (a Puerto Rican dish similar to a tamale) for Christmas, but other than that, celebrating with food was not a major concern in my upbringing or in my home with my husband and children.

Staying away from red meat was easy for us, as we were not big red-meat eaters to begin with. When I was pregnant with my son twenty-six years ago, I walked into the kitchen and became nauseated from the hamburger meat cooking. That was the last time I cooked or ate red meat. However, my husband and I enjoyed the "pernil" (pork) plate with rice and beans from the nearby mall. We looked forward to that on Sundays. Our usual dinner was chicken—broiled and overcooked. (I was always making sure I was "killing the salmonella!" But really, I was just a lousy cook.) I was never a "fryer." I thought frying food was too unhealthy to begin with and, to be honest, I really did not like the mess it made on the stove.

Staying away from cakes and cookies was also pretty easy for me to do. I had always wanted my children to grow up coming home to that baked apple pie smell coming from the oven, but when I started to make a dessert one day and saw the amount of butter it required, I could not do it. The thought of all that butter in our food kind of made me disgusted and averse to baking, and so my children did not come home to the smell of apple pie. We would, however, buy one occasionally from the store.

After a while, the sugar was easy for me to give up. I would always get headaches behind my eyes if I had too much sugar, and too much sugar was just a few cookies. I never felt right after eating sugary treats, so it really was easy to give them up. We were, however, junk food junkies. Chips Ahoy! were a favorite. We loved M&M'S with Doritos. My children were treated to McDonald's, Burger King, and Kentucky Fried Chicken. We have come a long way from those days. Now our snacks are lentil chips with celery, carrot sticks with hummus, nuts, fruit, smoothies, and, recently, a delicious health bar made with dates and walnuts. My daughter usually prepares the bars. I love when I open the fridge and find a pan of them just sitting there waiting to be eaten.

Breakfast had always consisted of Frosted Flakes and milk for my husband, and oatmeal for me. Lipton tea was my beverage of choice. I had been drinking hot tea since I was a little girl. My father served it in the mornings. I had often joked with my children that they should put a Lipton tea bag in my casket for me.

Lunch was chicken sandwiches with mayonnaise, leftover chicken with rice and beans from the night before, or Lean Cuisine frozen dinners. Rice and beans was a popular dish in our house. If we had any vegetables, it was iceberg lettuce, cucumbers, and tomatoes. Frozen vegetables occasionally appeared on our dinner table.

We started out in our marriage thirty-three years ago rather poor. We remember rummaging through our coats to find change to buy milk for the kids. Even to add green pepper to the beans seemed too expensive. Ketchup became my substitute for the tomato sauce that was too expensive. Healthy eating was not top priority back then—neither was cooking.

As time went on, I developed acid reflux. I would wake up coughing at night from the gases, and seemed to always have stomach issues. I went for an endoscopy and a colonoscopy to rule out any cancer or ulcers. The diagnosis was that I had a flap that did not close and that allowed the gases to come back up. I was told to sleep sitting up, not eat close to bedtime, and take one pill a day. The doctor said it was probably something I was eating, but he offered no recommendations, and I could not figure out what the problem food was that I was eating. I hated taking that pill, but I felt like I had no other choice.

I had taken acid reflux medicine for ten years. Never did I expect what ended up happening.

Three weeks after I cut meat and dairy from my diet, I no longer needed to take that little pill each night. I no longer had acid reflux. Needless to say, I was overjoyed. It was an amazing feeling to know that because I changed my diet, I did not have to take that pill. I wondered why doctors did not recommend this. I figured they just did not know.

I was so excited that I wrote a letter to my gastroenterologist (my stomach doctor) and told him my story and how I no longer needed to be on medication. I thought he would be excited, curious, and want to know more. I thought he would be thrilled to be able to share this with his patients. He could tell them how they could cure their own acid reflux.

But he never wrote back.

At some point, I no longer enjoyed the taste of Lipton tea and other staple foods in my diet. My body certainly was telling me it wanted something different.

My family and I started to change our eating habits with transition foods, foods that are mostly processed but that made the switch to a plant-based diet a little easier: Tofurky fake meat slices, meatless meatballs, and non-chicken nuggets (to name a few). This was all food made to be substitutes for meat but made without the use of animal products. It was a good feeling knowing that I was eating healthier than I had been.

And it was an excellent substitute for what we were used to. We could have our traditional rice and beans, meatless meatballs and spaghetti, macaroni and "cheez," sandwiches, Tofu Pups (instead of hot dogs), and meatless ribs that you just need to heat up in the microwave—very delicious! (I no longer use a microwave, but that's another story.)

Luckily, I befriended a woman named Elizabeth who offered plant-based cooking lessons. She belonged to a Seventh-day Adventist church that had events to help educate the public on plant-based cooking. She was such a blessing! She taught me how to cook stuffed shells so delicious they even fooled "real" Italians, who could not tell they were made with tofu instead of dairy cheeses. She came to my house during the summer to teach me how to cook. At the age of forty-eight, I discovered the difference between a teaspoon and a tablespoon. She gave me an apron and my very own notebook to put my recipes in. There will always be a special place in my heart for Elizabeth!

I learned what kale was—and all the other vegetables that I had only seen but knew nothing about—as she led me through the aisles of the supermarket. (I've since learned that kale is the top vegetable in nutritional value. We eat it often, either juiced with carrots, apple, and lemon or other fruits and veggies, or sautéed with onions and garlic.) Roasted Brussels sprouts and roasted cauliflower have also become favorites of mine. That is a long way from pizzas and TV dinners.

Restaurants no longer had what I was willing to eat. Our favorite plant-based restaurant, Candle Cafe, was an hour away in New York City, and my small town offered nothing for my new diet. I was fortunate, however, to have a small natural food store twelve minutes from my house. They had the nutritional yeast flakes that I was now experimenting with in recipes to create a cheesy flavor. Macaroni and "cheez" was one of our favorites. They also had tofu and fake meats and cheeses, flax seeds, tamari, nondairy milks, and many other ingredients needed for our new lifestyle. They had what we needed for the recipes in our plant-based cookbooks, and offered a nice selection of organic vegetables. And they had Amy's dairy-free pizza! I absolutely loved Amy's pizzas!

I loved sharing my food. Loved, loved sharing my food. (Okay, my daughter cooked it—but I shared it!) At my retirement dinner, my friend Christine asked everyone to raise their hands if at some point I had tried to feed them some of my food, and almost the whole room raised their hands. Yes, I loved sharing my food. I wanted people to see how delicious my way of living was. I certainly did not eat lettuce all day like people imagined I did. Our diet was a far cry from what people thought.

Whenever we went out to visit friends, we would make sure we brought our own food. People felt bad that they could not feed us, but I did not mind bringing food. My stuffed shells and bean dip were super hits!

My daughter, who happened to start a plant-based diet before I had made the change, decided at this time that she was interested in going to cooking school. She enrolled and learned plant-based cooking at the Natural Gourmet Institute in New York City.

I was thrilled! I learned a little along with her. She taught me how to cut an onion and garlic without cutting my fingers off or taking forever! She taught me how to use a knife properly. She still wants me to trust my intuition when I cook, to just go with what feels right, but I am attached to using recipes. Too many years of fast food and heating things up in the oven hurt my freedom to experiment. I do look forward to becoming more comfortable in the kitchen, but it is taking time. My daughter still cooks for the family. I am really blessed to have her. What I really look forward to is having restaurants nearby that serve the food that I will eat—plant-based, organic, healthy. One day.

My whole family—my husband, my two children, and I—had changed to a total plant-based diet (no animal products) and became very health-conscious. We became aware of what was going in and on our bodies, from the food that we ate to the toothpaste and lotions we used. We read labels, shopped in health food stores, and looked carefully at the preparation of our food.

I was eating and treating my body the way that I wanted. My body adjusted to wanting more veggie dishes and less processed foods. The need for transition foods was ending for me; however, my husband loved his "bologna" and "cheez" sandwiches. It was not easy living in a meat and dairy society with the changes we were making, but the food situation got easier as time went on.

Deliciously,

Shanti

No Turning Back Now

Dear World,

No, there was no turning back now. We had learned too much already. I read books and books on health advice. *The China Study* greatly influenced my thinking and the way I saw things. The author, T. Colin Campbell, PhD, performed experiments on lab rats. He gave them a cancer-causing agent and then discovered he was able to increase and decrease cancer with the amount of animal protein he gave the rats. Five percent animal protein would not promote the cancer. Five percent animal protein is the same as eating two chicken nuggets a day.[7] That would mean no milk, cheese (or anything else with dairy in it), and no meat of any kind for the rest of the day, or it had the potential to turn on cancer. This fascinated me! How could we not know this? Why was this the total opposite of what I had been taught growing up?

When I talk to people about nutrition, some talk about the paleo diet, which relies heavily on meat, as a diet that makes sense to them. Based on Campbell's research, the paleo diet does not make sense to me when I look at all the moral, physical, and environmental reasons to change to a plant-based diet.

At fifty-three, my husband's yearly checkup shows him to be in great health, and he has lost sixty pounds—forty pounds almost immediately and the other twenty slowly but surely. He saw a dramatic change when he drank water instead of soda. I find that my body craves the veggies and gets really upset with me when I eat the things that are processed or have sugar in them. No more honey-dipped donuts from Dunkin' Donuts for me. No more cinnamon rolls from the deli with bacon, egg, and cheese and a bottle of Coke for my husband.

But, seven years later, we are both in our fifties and in great health. I like that trade. We ate healthy. We became healthy. Very nice feeling. I will be that little old lady dancing on stage at one hundred years old after all! Every time I see a commercial for acid reflux, I appreciate that it is not part of my life anymore. There is no need for medication for any of us! We now consider food our medicine. Anytime anyone is feeling a cold coming on (and it does not happen very often), out comes the juicer!

Last year, when my husband and I had our yearly physicals, our doctor said how nice it was to have back-to-back checkups for two healthy people. She did not usually see that. I lent her the *Forks Over Knives* DVD. She was curious about how to help her plant-based patients. I love my doctor!

Life was all about learning how to be healthy—cooking and eating healthy. *The China Study* was an amazing study on preventing cancer. And it was one of those books that I was not used to reading. I was used to reading teachers' books and children's books, not books about scientific studies. But I loved it. I read a book by Caldwell Esselstyn Jr., MD, called *Prevent and Reverse Heart Disease*, saw videos on reversing diabetes, read how a plant-based diet can make you live longer, and more! I was thrilled. I knew I was treating my body well. I could not learn enough or fast enough!

* * *

I wanted to share such incredible information with people, but they stayed away from me. I think they felt guilty being around me. My husband said that they felt judged by me. It was hard for me to understand why people were not taking better care of themselves or why they didn't want to learn how. I did not mean to judge. I just wanted better for them. It always amazed me that videos were returned with a "thank you," which was really a "thanks, but no thanks."

It was then that I started to realize I had not only been given a responsibility, but I had been given a gift—the gift of health.

I had to fight to learn how to survive, but here was a gift that people could have for free. They did not have to have a cancer scare. They did not have to be told that they had five years to live. This was a gift that did not cost them anything. Yet, they did not want it. I saw their pain, their aches, their diseases, and I saw them choose sickness instead of health. I was frustrated. I did not understand, and it made me sad.

Caringly,

Shanti

Loving Animals

Dear World,

I have always loved animals.

I never wanted to see any of them hurt. The only time I ever cut class in high school was when they were going to dissect a frog. I just could not bear the thought of cutting an animal open. It was worth cutting class. I'd do it again. Only this time, I would get everyone else to cut class with me!

When I was a little girl, my family had a little Chihuahua, Muñeco ("doll" in Spanish). We had so much fun playing with him. He had such personality. My father taught him how to take a dollar out of his pocket. We took him for rides in the doll stroller and treated him just like a baby. He *was* our baby. We loved Muñeco. And he was a doll. But, oh my goodness, not at night. He would turn into this mean old, grumpy thing. He would sleep at the foot of my bed and bite my feet if I moved while I slept. Obviously he did not want to be disturbed by anyone while he slept. I think it is funny now to look back and see what I allowed. But we loved him. He definitely was a member of our family.

As a married couple, the first dog my husband and I got was a German shepherd mutt. We lived in Hawaii when we adopted her. We named her Kila. In Hawaiian it means "strong" or "bold." She was strong and bold—and smart. I remember fondly how she managed to wiggle her way out of her harness, run down the road to the school where I was teaching, and run into my classroom of twenty surprised and excited children! Sister Joan, the principal, was not so excited.

Kila was not a vocal dog, not a barker at all! However, there once was a strange man who had been lurking around the neighborhood. Kila barked for the first time when she saw this man come up the road. I always wondered what she knew that we did not (because she obviously knew more than we did about certain things). She was a great dog. I miss her.

I always loved animals of any kind. I thought owning them was our way of showing love, and since my kids were allergic to cats and dogs, we decided to get an iguana. We made a closet into a house for her. (My husband says I speak French when I use "we." He actually does all the handyman work around the house. I just speak French.) So anyway, "we" made a corner cage made out of plexiglass and placed a shelf, wood shavings, and a branch inside for her. We would take her out of her house to play and, without fail, she would do her business on the couch where I'd put her. I always hoped she would not do that, but, as I look back, I guess she did not want to dirty her cage.

She was fun to have. She was a unique pet. But we did not know how to take care of this animal, as much as we thought we did. It was sad when she died. (We didn't even know if she was actually female. We just called her a girl because my daughter gave her a girl's name.)

After the iguana died, we put a ball python in the cage. He scared me. We had to feed him baby mice. It was sad when he caught them. I did not like having him. I did think he was super cool, though. I really liked the intrigue of having him. We showed him off to all of our guests. But as much as we thought we knew how to take care of him, we didn't.

Keeping these animals from having the lives they were meant to have was not a very good way to show our love for them. They did not belong in my closet. I thought they did. I did not consider that they could have their own lives in the wild. They certainly had no life in my closet.

I look back now and regret having kept them from their natural habitats. Allowing them to remain in their habitats would have been love. But for sure, no matter what, I was always an animal lover.

And yet, I had never made the connection between the animals that I loved so dearly and the animals I called my food.

From an animal lover,

Shanti

A Rude Awakening

Dear World,

As I continued to learn about my diet and healthy eating, I read *Diet for a New America* by John Robbins, and I knew I would never ever eat meat or dairy products *ever* again. Not because of my health, but because of the animals that I was eating. The author talked about the animals that I had been calling food like they were real and had feelings and personalities. I had not seen that before.

It took me three months to read that book. I could only absorb a little bit at a time, cry, and then put it away for a while. My husband kept asking me why I read it if it made me so upset. Time and time again, I said that I had to. I just knew that I had to continue. Little did I realize that by reading and learning about the animals, I was gaining strength.

Scenes in the *Earthlings* documentary still haunt me. Any time I see someone wearing fur, I immediately think of the scenes in that film—scenes of pain, brutality, and death. They are forever etched in my brain. And when I see someone eating a hamburger, I do not see food. I see pain. I see terror.

I want you to see what I see. Not because I want you to experience the pain that I feel, but because I want you to see the things that we, as a society, do. And perhaps you will care about it enough to make a difference. And if you think that one person can't make a difference, that your choices are too small to make a difference, try sleeping with a mosquito in your room. That little mosquito would surely make your night difficult! No one is too small to make a difference.

We have to see the connection and we have to care. We have to see what we, as a society, do to the living beings on Earth, because then, as a society, we can choose compassion. And if we are open to understanding the karmic connection, we can choose to not live with all the violence, depression, and devastation in our home, planet Earth.

I continued to gain strength by watching DVDs like *Earthlings* and other videos showing animal torture. I became angry. It strengthened me. I became obsessed with wanting to do something. I knew someone had to help. I felt that I had to. It was a responsibility that I had been given. I was confused as to why people were not inspired by the words, "thou shalt not kill," and why they did not apply it to all beings. I could not understand how people could commit such horrible acts to animals.

And horrible, unimaginable things *are* happening. The horror continues to drive me. In writing this book, I have chosen not to be descriptive about the abuse. Too many of you would put the book down and not continue reading. I want you to keep reading.

* * *

I started to live my life doing the least amount of harm possible to any animal. I read labels to make sure they did not contain any animal products. I looked online to make sure the products that I used were not tested on animals. I could not deal with the atrocious ways we scientifically experiment on them. I looked at clothing labels to make sure they did not have wool or silk or animal fur. The humane ways we would like to envision fur and wool being taken from the animals simply is not reality. The leather industry is quite a cruel one also. Try Googling where we get our leather from in India. That is a sad story. Americans' image of India is that they are kind and compassionate toward cows because the cows are sacred. Not so. Find out where leather comes from. Very sad.

My leather sneakers were the last animal-derived product that I gave up. In meditation class one day, the teacher asked us to take energy and push it out of our bodies, but the energy got stuck in my feet. I knew what that meant. After class, I went straight to Target and bought a new pair of sneakers—man-made.

I continued to watch videos from the national nonprofit organization Mercy For Animals—videos taken by undercover investigators in concentrated animal feeding operations (CAFOs). I guess these are what can be called the "new version" of Old MacDonald's farm—buildings where our animals are being raised to be slaughtered. The videos' contents were not nice. They were horrendous. They were cruel and inhumane and they left me crying for days.

And I had to share this information with everyone. Once again I wanted to stand on the mountaintops and shout to the world. Yes, I wanted them to change, but more than that, I wanted them to see. Because once they saw, they would want to change for themselves.

Or so I thought. It was happening all over again! People did not want to hear about health, and now they didn't want to hear about the animals.

And then the comments and jokes would start: "You know the definition of a vegetarian? Lousy hunter." Ha, ha, ha. And they would laugh. And I would hurt.

At a Toastmasters meeting, after one of my vegan speeches, another member came up to me and said, "I also support veganism. I am a member of PETA—people who eat tasty animals." And I had to act as if that did not hurt. I had to hold my tongue. I wanted to take him by the shoulders and shake him and say, "Don't you see the cruelty that happens so you can have your tasty animals?" But I did not say anything. I tried very hard not to offend people. It hurt me when people did not care and then, on top of it, made jokes. I tried very hard not to be an "angry vegan." It would not have helped.

I bought multiple copies of videos and offered them to many people. I wanted everyone to see them. I wanted everyone to know what was happening. I thought they would care like I did. But they did not. Many people would not even watch the videos. They said it was too painful to see such things; they did not want to get upset. I did not understand why they did not see the connection—that they were asking someone to kill for them so that they could eat, that the animals suffering in the videos were suffering because of them. But I stayed quiet. I was trying very hard not to offend people. And I definitely have no intention of offending anyone as I write this.

Some people would watch the videos, but decide a vegan lifestyle was too difficult. I could not understand how seeing this suffering did not convince people to change their eating habits.

People had lots of reasons for why they chose to argue against the vegan point of view. "We were meant to be meat eaters." "We have canine teeth." "I eat venison; it is so much healthier than other meat." "I need my protein." "I don't feel good when I don't eat meat." "We are on top of the food chain, and that is just the way it was meant to be!" "God meant for it to be this way. He gave us animals to eat!" I hated when they pulled the "God card."

I was frustrated. I did not know how to speak to people so that they would understand, and so I got quiet. I did not get quiet in my head, though. I was angry and frustrated and I said an awful lot, but it stayed in my head. I did not want to offend. I did not want to give people a reason to hate me just because of what I stood for.

A common remark I heard many times was, "God gave us dominion over animals. He gave them to us to eat." To which I would reply (many times in my head), "God did not give us animals to brutalize and kill. He gave them to us to care for, not to do what we do to them."

One person questioned, "Why are animals here if they are not here for our food?" I hope she reads this book.

Or some people would say, "It is too hard to live that lifestyle. I go out too much and it would hurt my social life." To which I would reply (probably in my head), "You think you would be inconvenienced? Just think of what the animals go through. You think they are not inconvenienced?"

Or they would say, "Everything in moderation." And my smart aleck self definitely would say, "Everything? Even crack?" You cannot give out pain in moderation. You can either allow violence or not.

And some people would patronizingly say, "Good for you. I wish I had your passion." To which I would reply (in my head, once again), "You would care if you knew. You would have my passion."

Because I was offending people, I had learned to just respond in my head. They did not want anything to do with me. It was too difficult for them. And you know, I really did understand the fact that it was our culture, that it was the way we were brought up. It was tradition. I really did understand that. That is the way I was raised, too.

Communication just didn't seem to be working with the people in my circle. It was at this time when people really stopped talking to me. I was upsetting many, many people by trying to tell them about the horrendous things that were happening to animals. They simply did not want to hear about it. They wanted to eat their meat and did not want to hear about the reality of the situation.

My husband claimed that I "preached." I just wanted people to see what was happening. What I was learning was not a religion. It was the reality of pain. It was the reality of torture. It was the reality that our actions were causing this. Religion? Religion gives us reasons to love, not torture and kill.

I cared. I cared to tears. Many, many tears.

* * *

I had joined Toastmasters, my public-speaking support group, to learn communication and leadership skills. I needed to learn how to get this message out so people would understand without feeling offended.

People needed to hear and understand veganism. I was now a vegan.

I now chose to live my life doing the least amount of harm possible to any animal, and I wanted others to choose it also.

It was then that I saw another gift. I was given the gift of veganism—of consciousness, of being mindful of the connection between the suffering involved in raising animals for food and pleasure, and the creation of a peaceful and compassionate world. It is all about karma.

Respectfully,

Shanti

Vegan Activism

Dear World,

My new life can be summed up with this anonymous quotation popular in the vegan community: "Never, never be afraid to do what's right, especially if the well-being of a person or animal is at stake. Society's punishments are small compared to the wounds we inflict on our soul when we look the other way."

I was choosing to do what was right, especially since the well-being of an animal was at stake. The well-being of billions of animals was at stake.

Some people did look, see, and adjust their lifestyles. My best friend, Christine, changed to a vegan diet after sitting with me at lunch every day for two years and hearing me talk. You can only imagine what it must have been like for her to go through what she went through with me. But in the end, she saw. She shared with me that she did not want to see. She knew in the back of her mind that horrible things were happening, but she did not want to know because once she knew, she would have to do something. She would have to change, and change seemed impossible to her—much too difficult, and very scary.

I began to actively work to get the vegan message out. I needed people to see. I needed them to care enough to do something. Many people were touched and did care. I am grateful for the people who saw, felt, and then changed their lifestyles. They have joined the 2–3 percent of the United States population that are vegan.[8] However, that means over 300 million people in the United States are meat eaters. Three hundred million people in the United States alone did not know or just did not care.

I had to speak to the people who cared. I continued to

believe that everyone would care.

I handed out pamphlets about veganism at all sorts of events—fairs, dinners, farmers markets. Wherever I could put a pamphlet, I did. It was fun putting them in the bathroom at Home Depot. I often wondered who picked them up and what their reaction was. I wondered if they got angry and threw it away. I prayed that it would be found by someone who would care like I did.

I read books. I saw videos. I spoke to anyone I could about the animal abuse. This became an obsession. It seemed to define who I was. I was okay with that. My husband was not quite so sure. I wanted to become a billboard and wear my vegan T-shirts everywhere. My husband was not too thrilled. We compromised. When I was with him, I did not wear them. When I went out by myself, I could wear what I wanted. It is not like he eats meat. He also changed his diet and lives his life doing the least amount of harm possible. He just does not feel the need to share with other people like I did—like I do.

In a status update on the Facebook page for his blog, *The Thinking Vegan*, Gary Smith expressed my sentiments exactly:

> You know how much you love, respect and want to protect every dog and cat in the world? You know how much your heart breaks when you see a picture of a dog in a shelter who is going to be killed? You know how you feel when you see photos of piles of dead dogs and cats who are going to be used for fur? You know how enraged you get when you see a photo of a dog or cat who has been beaten to death? That's how vegans feel about all animals. Every animal who is exploited and murdered for food, clothing, entertainment and "research." We don't distinguish between dogs and cats and other animals. If you allowed yourself to feel the deep suffering that billions of animals endure for your pleasure, you'd be vegan, too. And you might understand why vegans work so hard to end

the animal holocaust.[9]

Yes, that is exactly how I feel, and have felt for the past seven years. And it was difficult! Sometimes I screamed, I cried, I wondered in disbelief. I wanted to shake people to get them to understand. Yet they did not. And I felt helpless. But I knew I had to keep doing something.

Sometimes I think
it's better to live in the dark
yet I seek the light
though it hurts my heart and blinds my eyes.
—Whitney Metz[10]

* * *

I attended Vegetarian Summerfest in Johnstown, Pennsylvania, a yearly event that has speakers, food, entertainment, and, above all, classes and workshops. It was at this event that I felt the thrill of gaining knowledge. This information was so exciting to learn about: the health aspects, the food demonstrations, the planet connection, the books, the animal lectures. And I met people who had lived their whole lives as vegans! After the conference, I remember saying that this was the feeling that I wanted my students in school to leave with each day—the thrill of learning.

At this festival, I picked up a flyer to attend a retreat in Michigan hosted by Dr. Will Tuttle, author of the bestseller, *The World Peace Diet.* In preparation to go to this retreat, I read his book.

My eyes were opened. Not only had I seen the health, the animal, and the planet connection to being vegan, but I now also saw the spiritual connection, the Golden Rule connection, the karmic connection.

I learned what compassion meant. In *The World Peace*

Diet, Dr. Tuttle writes, "Compassion is ethical intelligence: it is the capacity to make connections and the consequent urge to act to relieve the suffering of others."[11] I had that on a magnet on my fridge for years. I read it over and over.

I had to act to relieve the suffering of others.

For the animals,

Shanti

A Reverence for Life

Dear World,

I have a drawer full of T-shirts, buttons, and bumper stickers, all with vegan messages and quotes from famous people. My fridge had a bumper sticker on it for a while that said, "Friends don't let friends drink milk." Yes, I certainly made myself a billboard for veganism whenever I could get away without the rolling eyes of my husband! (I appreciate him. I probably would have been arrested a long time ago for some protest or another. But then again, that might not have been so bad!)

I have a T-shirt with a quote from Paul McCartney in PETA's video, *Glass Walls*. It says, "If slaughterhouses had glass walls, we would all be vegetarian."[12] And I have found that to be true, but not always. Not everyone would be vegetarian. A friend of ours watched all the videos that I gave him. For a while he changed his diet, mostly for his health, but then went back to eating whatever was the easiest. It made me sad. I wondered why the awareness of animals' suffering did not seem to matter to him. The last time I saw him, he had gained at least fifty pounds.

Anyway, some of the buttons, T-shirts, and bumper stickers had quotes by Albert Schweitzer. The quotes fascinated me so much that I read up about him. He has become one of my favorite people, along with John Lennon, Gandhi, Buddha, Jesus, and Amos Lee. Schweitzer helped people with malaria, severe diarrhea, and leprosy in the deep parts of Africa for almost his whole life. He was a brilliant man: a doctor, philosopher, theologian, musician, and Nobel Peace Prize winner.

This book, *Dear World, See What I See*, is based on his philosophy of "a reverence for life." Reverence for life comes from his thoughts and writings about our will to live. We all want to live. Every living being wants to live, from plants to bears, and, of course, us. We share this with every living thing. And because we all have this will to live, we owe all other living things the same care and respect that we want for ourselves. [13]

Our society needs to be open to seeing the consequences of *not* having this reverence for life, of not being in awe of the mystery of life.

I hope you begin to see how each one of us can change things to make a better world if we choose, if you find that this book makes some sense to you.

Albert Schweitzer died in 1965 without getting his message heard. People were too busy fighting and holding on to their steadfast ways to consider living a compassionate life and, possibly, a way to peace. I wonder if we are still too busy.

I recently entered a Toastmasters contest with a speech that I worked on for two months. It was, as someone told me, "a piece of art." It was a speech about the idea of this book. I lost the contest. Few people's mouths hung open as I placed last. Well, almost last. The last place person was disqualified because he spoke over the time limit. My speech was absolutely incredible. It was compelling. It was professionally spoken, and I did not miss a beat in the delivery. Why did I place last? I am not sure. I walked away wondering if people are not ready or if it was just going to take a lot more than a seven-minute speech to inspire them to live more compassionate lives. Perhaps the time that it takes to read this book will do it. I am hoping.

I love Toastmasters. They have helped me find my voice and express myself. I cannot say enough good things about the organization and the members of my club. When I first started to give speeches and would say things like, "There is pus in milk," I was told that I could not speak like that because they stopped listening to me. They shut me down. It was too hard for them to hear. So I have continued in Toastmasters for four years attempting to speak so people hear me and do not shut me out. I love the skills that I've gained in my club.

As I have come to hear from others, Toastmasters was not the place to take this serious message, unless I could make it entertaining. Perhaps that will be my new challenge: looking at the humorous side of my life as a vegan. How much funnier could it get than going to a restaurant for a birthday celebration at a club and being given a separate table because we did not eat the "normal" meal? My family and I thought it was funny. Society separated us because we don't eat animals. That is funny.

Humanity is not in awe. We don't see life and marvel at its wonder. We kill it and eat it. We perform science projects on it. We confine it and make it do what we want it to do. Being in awe of the mystery of life would mean to allow life to be. To marvel at it. To observe it and be amazed at its complexities. How did we get here? How does a frog bury himself in the mud all winter and survive? How do male penguins survive all winter in frigid temperatures holding an egg on their feet? How do dolphins and whales help people in distress in the middle of the ocean? We don't live in awe. We kill whatever moves.

Many species have gone extinct, many because of man's doing. And we are just another species that we are endangering. Will we put ourselves on the endangered species list one day? Did you know that animal agriculture is destroying the environment? The earth will not be able to sustain us any longer if we continue to do what we are doing. And we are doing it in the name of our food. Kind of an oxymoron—we need our food, but our food is killing us.

Peace,

Shanti

You Are What You Eat

Dear World,

I wrote a poem:

You are what you eat.
You eat terror. You eat fear. You eat the energy that is in that animal.
There are no happy cows when they are taken to be slaughtered.
There are no painless, "Gee, I did not realize I am being killed"
slaughterhouses.
At the end of a tortured, depressed, hopeless life, the animals' lives are
ended in fear and in terror.
It is the energy of fear and terror that is coursing through their bodies.
Then we eat their bodies.
You are what you eat.

The common saying, "You are what you eat," makes sense. Doctors will tell you that you are what you eat. They refer to it from the standpoint of health. If you eat a lot of fat, chances are that plaque will build up in your arteries, and blood won't pump through your body as easily. Heart disease will follow. They'll put you on medication. It is easy to see how you are what you eat. But there is also the emotional side to what you eat.

How much of the violence that each person has in their emotional state can we link back to what we eat? How much hopelessness is in the animals' cells? How much sadness and desperation did the animals live with and you eat? I think each person will have to answer for themselves.

Some might say, "I am eating the spirit of that animal! It is a good thing!"

I say, "When you are hurting, when you are frustrated, when you are in pain, doesn't your spirit hurt?" The animals' spirits are hurting. Why would you want to eat the spirits of animals that are hurting?

Can we continue to live our lives knowing that we are not only hurting another being, but that we are also hurting ourselves—our physical and emotional selves—for the sake of our taste buds?

You are what you eat.

Deep regards,

Shanti

Planet Connection

Dear World,

I belong to the vegan community, so I receive many e-mails and Facebook messages regarding vegan issues. I've also read and seen many pamphlets, booklets, books, and videos on vegan issues. As I started to read facts about the earth, something struck me hard when it came to the oceans: scientists say that by the year 2048 there will be no more sea life if we continue to do what we are doing to the oceans.[14] And you may ask, "What scientists? How can you prove that?"

And I say, "Let's be concerned. If scientists are really correct, then we are destroying the very life that is in our oceans. What are we doing?"

Google "ocean fishing nets," and learn about the miles-long nets that scoop whatever is in their paths from the ocean, with the majority of the catch going to feed cows.[15] I just Googled it. There is plenty of information for you there.

Not only are we allowing horrible atrocities to happen, but we are also on the brink of losing our planet. Yes, the planet will be around for a long time; however, *we* may not be. The planet may not be healthy enough to sustain us, to give us clean water, fresh air, and edible food. We won't be able to live here, nor will the millions of animal species be able to survive with what humanity is doing. No, we do not live in awe. And we are going to pay for it.

Hopefully, other civilizations will come (granted, with their own problems and lifestyles), but do we really want to be the civilization that could have made a healthier planet for them and chose not to? Our behavior right now is the deciding factor.

* * *

I live in a beautiful suburb of New York. I run my faucet, and I get clear, drinkable water. I flip a switch, and my lights turn on. I open my fridge, and it is filled with delicious food. I look outside, and the grass is green and the trees and bushes are lush and the air is fresh. Everything seems perfect.

I grew up spoiled with the comforts of life. My children have grown up with the comforts of life. We never had to worry about not having water, food, or fresh air.

But the world is large and not everywhere is as comfortable or as fortunate. And because of our increasing demand for animal products, we are destroying what many of us have taken for granted—clean air, water, and food. I see it in the pond that I grew up going to each summer, where we could safely jump in and take a swim. The lake water was fresh and beautiful. Today it saddens me to see frothy, smelly water that I would not dream of swimming in.

Our environment may become so harsh to live in, as it is for the majority of animals on our earth, that we humans may find it difficult to survive.

And we are doing this—destroying our planet—because of our incredible "need" to have animals be our food and our choice to not see the consequences of our actions.

I say it's time to see. If neither health reasons nor animal reasons convinced you to think about your food choices, then perhaps planetary reasons might. After all, we do need our planet to exist.

One-third of our planet is used to the raise animals.[16] (And I use the term "raise" very loosely. Raising is not what I think of when I think of the care that we give to our animals.) Being the elementary school teacher that I was, I picture a pie split into three sections. It is mindboggling to think that one-third of that pie, of our earth, is given to raising livestock for food. And each day that piece of the pie is growing larger and larger.

It is hard to imagine huge numbers. In 2009, fifty-nine

billion animals worldwide died for food.[17] Fifty-nine billion. It is hard to see it. David Schwartz, author of the children's book *How Much Is a Million?*, says, "If you sat down to count from one to one billion, you would be counting for 95 years."[18] And we killed *fifty-nine billion* in one year! Those billions of animals need a place to live, a place to graze, plus all of the farmland that is required to grow food to feed them—one-third of our planet. That's crazy!

The acres of forest that are cut down per minute around the world for the animals is unbelievable. As I sit here, there are trees being cut to allow for the grazing of the animals, animals that will be fattened and shipped to the United States for meat eaters to eat—a contribution to the destruction of our planet.[19] I saw a post on Facebook from Greenpeace's Tumblr page that said, "The Earth is 4.6 billion years old. Scaling to 46 years, humans have been here for 4 hours. The Industrial Revolution began 1 minute ago, and in that time, we've destroyed more than half the world's forests."[20] We are destroying the lungs of our planet.

Seventy percent of the grain grown in the United States is used by the meat industry.[21] All of that grain could go to feed the world. Hunger could end. We don't have to have starving people in this world! Did you know that? I didn't. I just thought there was not enough food for them. The grain that goes to feed animals for our food could go to feed the world.

People around the world hate Americans for our greed, for taking more of the earth than we should. It makes you wonder. It sounds like we do take more than our fair share. And it makes sense to me that we are hated for taking grain away from starving people and giving it to cows for our dinner.

According to the United States Department of Agriculture, one acre of land can grow twenty thousand pounds of potatoes. But when used to grow cattle feed, that same acre of land produces less than 165 pounds of edible meat.[22] It makes compassionate sense to become a plant-based nation and share with the starving people of the world. That would make me a proud American.

When I was a little girl and I fussed about finishing my food, my mother would tell me, "Don't waste your food. There are people starving in Africa."

The child that I was would say, "Then send it to them 'cause I don't want it!" Little did I realize how true that could be. Instead of feeding our cows the grain, we could send the grain to hungry people. We would have so much if we did not give it to the animals—we certainly could share! We can live on a plant-based diet. And as creative as humans are, we certainly can make it taste really, really good. Vegan chefs make delicious food. I am proud my daughter is one!

A friend of mine says that she really knows. She knows it is the right thing to do, but she is a mother, and the mother in her worries that her daughter may not get the right nutrition if she stops eating meat and dairy. I understand. We were raised to believe that we need meat for protein and milk for strong bones. Keep learning. Go visit the sites listed in the notes section of this book. You will find that science does not back up the need for meat and dairy. She may be doing more harm to her daughter by insisting that she eat animal products.

Large land animals like elephants, giraffes, and hippopotami all live on a plant-based diet. Where do they get their protein? From the garden.

In regard to health, the only thing that a vegan absolutely needs to do is supplement with vitamin B_{12}.[23] Websites like nutritionfacts.org and pcrm.org are great places to learn about B_{12} and the other needs of your own body.

A few people have asked what would happen to all of the livestock. We impregnate them at staggering rates, but we can stop that horrendous practice and phase out the mass production of animals. This will not happen overnight. But if we can land on the moon, we are smart enough to figure out the logistics of phasing out the majority of the animals that we eat. We just have to be open enough to make a change.

Almost 50 percent of the water consumed in the United States is used by the meat industry.[24] One aquifer (underground water) in the Midwest, called the Ogallala Aquifer, which took over ten thousand years to form, has been drained so quickly in the past half century that we have begun to deplete it.[25] What will happen then? Clean water being scarce really is a reality. We don't need this. We don't have to be greedy with the earth. We don't have to let this happen. We can stop it. But we have to act now. All of us!

I love long showers. I feel guilty sometimes about using the water. Then I think of the fact that I could leave my shower running all year, nonstop, and still not use the amount of water a meat eater requires to raise his or her food.[26]

There are dead spots in the ocean—places where life can no longer exist because we've polluted them so badly with animal feces and other waste from livestock farms.[27] Are we crazy? What are we doing? I will be eighty-two when there will be no more sea life. I will still be here. That will be a sad time. I may not want to be that one hundred-year-old lady dancing on stage if things don't change.

Have you ever read the children's book *The Lorax*, by Dr. Seuss? (If you were in my class, you heard it.) I highly recommend it if you have not read it. Dr. Seuss saw. He wanted you to see. People are just too busy to look at what is really important. Dr. Seuss saw it years ago. Like Albert Schweitzer, he, I would imagine, also had to come to the realization that society was not ready for his message either.

The Food and Agriculture Organization of the United Nations' 2006 report, *Livestock's Long Shadow*, says that animal agriculture produces more greenhouse gases than all the transportation in the world.[28] That means the raising of animals is more dangerous than all the cars, buses, trucks, trains, and planes. Animal agriculture contributes significantly to global warming. So yes, buy that electric car. But it's far more important to stop supporting the animal industry.

We can do something, but we have to do something now. We can't wait any longer. Spread this message to your friends. Let this be a grassroots effort. Let us, the little people, change it. We can do something. We can choose a vegan diet. We can choose the right thing. Demand that we are fed a plant-based diet. Request that restaurants and grocery stores supply us with what we want. They will hear us—but we all have to speak.

Optimistically,

Shanti

Societal Karma

Dear World,

I have always heard the word "karma" and thought I knew what it meant. I had never really studied karma, but I thought it would keep me on the right path if I did not want bad things to happen to me. I've lived a pretty honest life. I have always valued honesty, no matter the consequences. I guess "karma" and being raised with good morals helped keep me on a virtuous path. Thanks, Mom and Dad (and while we are at it, thanks for naming me Shanti).

The concept of karma has been around for thousands of years. There are many different views of karma, including Hindu ideas and Western ideas. In general, the idea of karma is that doing good will bring good into your life, and doing bad will bring bad into your life.[29]

If you believe in karma, if you have a reason for living the Golden Rule, then you can see what I see.

You can see the connection.

Ancient teachings have spoken for many, many years about the Golden Rule: treat others as you want to be treated. Maybe we really did not understand why it was so important. We just knew it was a good way to live. For years we have taught the Golden Rule to our children. And through the years, we have even found different ways to say it: What goes around comes around. You reap what you sow. Live by the sword, die by the sword. That is karma.

It makes sense until we see good people who have had something bad happen to them. We get confused. Why did that happen to that person? He was a good person. He did not deserve what came to him. And when we don't understand why certain things happen, we don't believe in the Golden Rule anymore. And we don't live the Golden Rule. And we don't teach our children the Golden Rule.

And sometimes we get violent people.

In a way, violence is an unconscious act. Those who commit violence are not aware of its consequences, especially to themselves.

They don't know about karma.

Yes, bad things happen to good people and good things happen to bad people. So why is this karma thing so important? It doesn't seem to really work. But if we look at it in a different way, perhaps we can see that it *does* work, just not quite in the way we always thought. Perhaps there is more to it than individual karma. There is a spiritual and a scientific idea that all the beings of this earth are connected in some way—that we are one. Science, spirituality, and religions all agree that we are not separate, but that we are one. We are connected to all the beings on this planet by being the life on Earth.

So when we hurt another being, we are actually hurting ourselves. It's like the body. Your body has different parts, but is still one body. If you slam your finger in a door, not just your finger will be affected. Your whole body will be in agony. Your heart will race. And rightly so; your finger is part of you. In the same way, we are all separate individuals, yet we are connected. And since we are all connected, what I do to others is really hurting me.

Animals are also part of us. We are all life—*we* are the *beings* on Earth. We are connected to the animals just by being alive. They are part of us. So when we hurt the animals, we are also hurting ourselves.

Many people say, "Oh, I love animals. I treat my cats and dogs so well. I love them so much; I can't watch those sad ASPCA commercials on TV. It makes me sad to see animals treated that way."

Unfortunately, if you eat meat, you are asking someone to harm an animal for you. We love our cats and dogs dearly, but why love one and eat the other?

When we go to the store to buy food, we don't see animals. We see nicely packaged food in plastic wrapping, in cans, in jars, and at the deli counter. At some point, someone had to kill that animal for you.

And it was not a peaceful death—not at all. We don't see how that animal got packaged to be a nice, neat, inviting dinner.

At this point, some people may beg to differ with me. They might say that they definitely did not have anything to do with the cruelty inflicted on that animal.

If you were in a store with some friends and they stole some clothes from the store, who is guilty? Just the kids who actually took the clothing, or all of you? In the eyes of the law, all of you are guilty. All of you were going to enjoy the new clothes, or the money from them.

So when it comes to the abuse of the animals, you are going to benefit from the slaughter of that animal. You are going to have dinner.

At this point, I do hope that you understand and don't feel angry. I don't want to offend you. I just want you to see what I see. At one time in history, people considered it okay to have slaves. They were wrong. As a society, we could be wrong now. I want us to really become aware of what we are doing. Are we wrong now? How are our choices contributing to violence? We have to make a conscious decision and decide if this violence is something to which we want to contribute.

Perhaps it is not what each individual person does, but what we do as a society that comes back to us. Perhaps it is something like societal karma. Karma says what we give out, we will get back. And if we are all one, it does not seem to matter who gets it back—it seems to hit anyone. Perhaps that is why bad things happen to really good people.

* * *

Whether you believe in karma or not, there is no doubt that we are not treating the animals well.

And it's not right.

As a society, we confine, torture, and kill animals. We do it in the name of our food, our clothing, our entertainment, and our science. And we all benefit from the cruelty—from the food that is on our plates, to the leather sneakers and furniture that we own, to the circuses and zoos we enjoy, and to the products that we have in our homes.

Animals' natural reason for being on this earth is to live out the meaning of their lives—as we were meant to do. But we don't let the animals do that. We tell them how they are going to live, take away their homes, and do not allow them to be their true selves. We don't know what a gorilla wants, or a lion, or, for that matter, a chicken, a pig, or a cow. We do know that if a chicken had its choice, it would be nesting and digging and doing what chickens do. A pig would be digging with his snout and lying in the mud. And a cow would be grazing in the field with her babies. Yet, we look at them and think they are put on this earth for our needs and desires, then we put them through horrendous suffering just to serve our pleasures and our tastes.

My iguana and pet boa would not have chosen to live in my closet. I did not think about that back then.

If we put out violence, violence will come back to us. We look at news from our communities and around the world and wish people would stop their cruelty and violence. I think we should look at ourselves. As an elementary school teacher, I saw some children who did not get along with others and blamed everyone else. They took no responsibility for other children not liking them. They could not see what they were doing to create what was happening to them in their lives.

The violence that we impose on animals is coming back to

us. Cruelty is becoming our way of life. As we have become more violent toward other beings, more violence is coming back to us. We can see the increasing violence that is happening in our communities and around the world.

Our children cannot even go out to play in their own yards without fear of being bullied, kidnapped, or even killed. Violence is all you hear about on the news. It is happening out there. We all see it. Is this what we want for our lives? For our children? For generations to come?

We *can* do something about it. We *can* lessen violence. We *can* choose kindness. We *can* make a difference.

Karma says we can.

And for those who don't believe in karma, then how about compassion? How about our planet? How about your health? Pamela Rice, author of the pamphlet *101 Reasons Why I'm a Vegetarian*, gives you many more reasons. Please read it. You will be shocked at what you learn. Choose one reason to be vegan. It is important.

The goal of this book is to increase our level of awareness in order for us to do better. My hope is that you are open to this level of awareness. Please continue to learn.

See a little of what I see…please,

Shanti

Prayers Answered

Dear World,

December 21, 2012 came and went. According to the Mayan calendar, the world was supposed to come to an end. Obviously, that did not happen as some thought it would. I like to think that the world as we knew it came to an end and that a brand new consciousness, a new way of seeing things, began.

Do you believe in the power of prayer? And do you believe that prayers are answered? Many people do. The other day my friend Christine laughed at how her prayers were answered. She had prayed that people would be handing her checks. Well, they did—they handed her checks she was collecting for my retirement dinner! Some of us have heard the saying, "Be careful what you wish for because it might come true." The same goes for prayers. Prayers are answered, but God seems to have a sense of humor in how they are answered.

So many people pray for peace, especially at Christmas time. Perhaps this gift of peace is within our reach, yet we don't realize it. Perhaps we don't realize that the way to get peace is to be peaceful. Perhaps we have to do something first to receive the gift of peace. Perhaps we have to show we are worthy of peace. Gandhi said, "The greatness of a nation and its moral progress can be judged by the way its animals are treated."[30] Maybe we have to expect a higher standard from ourselves than the way we treat our animals now. Our moral progress needs to come into consciousness. Perhaps we are being judged—and it is not in our favor.

What do we have to do to be judged in a good light? We have to consider how we treat the other beings on this earth and choose to live with a higher moral standard. As animal rights activist Philip Wollen said in an interview with Gary Smith of

The Thinking Vegan blog, "I don't know why ethical people should fear the vegan tag. After all, it is the animal eater who should be ashamed. Without even seeking it, the vegan occupies the moral high ground. It is the vegan who is on the right side of history."[31]

Some people look at vegans and think that we have a "better than thou" attitude. We don't mean to come across that way. We just want to do the right thing for all. And we want you here with us.

Perhaps we have prayed so hard that peace really is ours for the taking. We just have to prove ourselves. We have to live better than we do.

Be peace and we will have peace. We have to stop asking someone to kill for us. We don't need to use animals to survive.

If we realize that we are the cause of our reality, perhaps we can understand that we can change our reality.

* * *

I just picked up a sharp kitchen knife. I held it in my hand and thought, "How angry, how heartless must someone be to stab another person or an animal with this?" I know I have felt angry, but angry enough to take someone's life? No, definitely not. But there are people out there who do that. They take a knife and take the life of another being. On top of all of the murders that occur in our communities, billions of land animals are slaughtered each year to become our food. The slaughterhouse workers live a life of mass murder for us. Like soldiers in a war, they go and kill without question. And they do it for us.

It is time for us to make the connection between what we do to others and what happens to us in our lives.

Gandhi said, "If we could change ourselves, the tendencies in the world would also change."[32] We have come to see those words as: "Be the change you want to see in the world."

If we want peace, we have to *be* peace. Peace is *not* asking someone to kill for us.

* * *

From the preface of C. David Coats's book, *Old MacDonald's Factory Farm*:

Absurdity

Isn't man an amazing animal? He kills wildlife—birds, kangaroos, deer, all kinds of cats, coyotes, beavers, groundhogs, mice, foxes, and dingoes—by the million in order to protect his domestic animals and their feed. Then he kills domestic animals by the billion and eats them. This in turn kills man by the million, because eating all those animals leads to degenerative—and fatal—health conditions like heart disease, kidney disease, and cancer.

So then man tortures and kills millions more animals to look for cures for these diseases. Elsewhere, millions of other beings are being killed by hunger and malnutrition because food they could eat is being used to fatten domestic animals. Meanwhile, some people are dying of sad laughter at the absurdity of man, who kills so easily and so violently, and once a year, sends out cards praying for "Peace on Earth."[33]

At the end of the day, at the end of my life, I have to say, "I lived my life causing the least possible amount of harm to any living being." It is the right thing to do—for me, for the animals, for my planet, for my spirit, and for the survival of mankind.

Sincerely,

Shanti

Stories of Karma in Life

Dear World,

In this letter, I share with you different stories where I see karma at work in my life—in our lives. Many times we look at life and shake our heads and wonder how some things could happen. I shake my head, too, and say, "It can only be that way. Karma says so."

There are so many times that I ponder life and see that connection. When you start to see what we do to animals, you also will start to see connections. From drug abuse, to obesity, to sickness, to desperation, to confinement, to apathy, to loneliness, to deceitfulness, to torture, to kidnapping, to the breaking up of families, you name it—we treat animals like that, so it only makes sense that it shows up in our lives.

No societies before lived like this. None were as cruel in so many different ways as we are to the enormous number of animals that we torture and kill. See what we do to animals. You will start to see those stories in your life, too.

* * *

Facebook is fun. You get to share your life with friends and learn a bit about their lives—the parties they go to, the friends they have, their families. Every once in a while people I don't know send me friend requests. What is it that these people want to friend me for? They like what I say? They like my posts? They saw my picture somewhere? I am not sure. Being on Facebook is sometimes a mysterious thing to me. (I am of the older generation that's not really sure how social media works.)

But anyway, why does someone want to friend me? That was the question I asked myself one day when a man with a name that was very difficult to pronounce sent me a friend request. I post interesting vegan information, so I thought he was interested in finding out more about it. We started talking through Facebook private messages and spoke on chat. He was very curious about my life. I was interested in learning about someone from another country. He tried to quote the Bible to me, and I tried to explain veganism to him. I thought it was fun to explain my position to someone I did not know. We talked now and then for about four months. He would ask for my phone number, tell me that he had to hear my voice. I told him no. He told me how much he loved me. I kind of laughed. I advised him to find someone to love who is *like* me—strong, honest, and smart.

And today I received a Facebook message from him telling me that his sister was in a really bad car accident, that he needed $2,000, and that he would pay me back. Really? I was supposed to believe that? And on top of that, the letter asking for the money was written by someone totally different than him. I was a teacher for twenty years. I know when someone else does your homework!

Here was someone whom I had had many honest conversations with, and he tried to take advantage of me! Deceit. Trickery. He tried to get one over on me.

And it makes sense. It's karma. That is what we do to our animals—we trick them. We put worms on a hook and try to trick the fish into getting caught. We set traps with cheese and peanut butter and hope the mice go for it. We set traps for bears, coyotes, foxes, deer, rabbits—we trick them all. Deceitful.

That Facebook friend showed what karma does. It goes around and comes around to whoever happens to be there. I happened to be there that time.

* * *

People are big these days. Me? I am five feet tall and just under one hundred pounds. But people are big. I don't mean to be critical, just observant.

We fatten broiler chickens so much that their skinny little legs can barely hold them up. Some just collapse because they can't carry their own weight around. Imagine being so fat that you couldn't walk. Some of us don't have to imagine that. We can truly feel their pain.

The chickens are selectively bred to make them as fat as possible, as fast as possible.[34] Because of this selective breeding, these chickens' lives are full of suffering. If these chickens were on their own, they would not be like this. But the fatter the chicken, the happier people are with their meat—and the happier the companies are with more money.

The food people eat makes them fat. When you eat milk, cheese, yogurt, and other dairy products, you are eating what a mother cow intended to give her baby. She wanted that baby calf to go from one hundred pounds at birth to twice that at just a month old. It only makes sense that this milk product is fattening. It is supposed to be.

On top of that, cheese and milk have casein in them. Casein is a milk protein that is addicting, like a drug.[35] That's why we love our cheese and always want more. Then we get fatter. And then we add addicting sugar and get fatter still.

I see really big people on TV all the time. I love *The Biggest Loser*, the show where people compete to see who can lose the most weight. It's an inspiring show for many people, but I feel bad for the people on the show. I wonder how they let themselves get that way.

And then I remember karma, and it all makes sense.

* * *

I meet so many women these days who are single, who just can't seem to meet a man whom they can fall in love with. For some reason there seems to be fewer men than women. My heart aches for their loneliness.

Then I think of karma, and I see it. What we do to pigs, cows, and chickens quite possibly is coming back to us.

Female chickens live their lives in cages.[36] (Egg-laying hens live disgusting lives.) Mother pigs are put in caged areas so small, they can barely move.[37] Dairy cows are kept pregnant and spend their lives hooked up to machines.[38] And they all do this without ever experiencing the joy of male companionship.

What goes around comes around. Very sad. And yet, it only makes sense.

* * *

I was thirty-two years old. I was home raising my two small children. I took different jobs to help my family financially. For three years, I worked nights as a waitress in a mall restaurant.

It was then that life took another turn.

I became friends with one of the cooks. He was a Bible-carrying, seemingly spiritual man. I was fascinated. I admired his knowledge.

He turned out to be an abusive person. He tricked me. He was, as they say, a wolf in sheep's clothing. He took advantage of my kindness, my naiveté, my thirst for knowledge. He then abused me.

Did I deserve that? Did I do something so bad in this life to have karma come back to me like that? I would like to think I did not. As a matter of fact, I *know* I did not. And then when I think about it, I realize I had been supporting the meat and dairy industry for over thirty years by that time. I am part of society. I have to take some responsibility also. I just happened to be the one that karma came back to in this way.

Societal karma. No one, good or bad, seems to be immune to the consequences.

What do we do to our cows and our pigs? We feed them. We pretend to care about them and then we rape them.

It only makes sense what happened to me. What goes around comes around. Karma.

You may wonder why and how I can put something so personal in this letter. It was an act of violence toward me. I am not embarrassed that someone was cruel enough to commit violence toward me. I did not choose the violence that he inflicted (at least not in this life). I have nothing to be ashamed of.

I am ashamed for not having known about veganism. I was the one who was contributing to violence. Not someone else.

* * *

The other day I went to a presentation by an author who is working on a story about her life after the death of her daughter. The author is a lovely lady. She had such a sweet voice and such a lovely smile on her face. She was mesmerizing. She shared the story of what happened during the days, weeks, and months that followed the death of her baby. Her daughter was twenty-eight years old, but her baby nevertheless. She loved her daughter with all her heart, as most mothers do. She talked about how smart, how full of life, and how precious her daughter was.

Mothers. There is such a bond that we have with our children. There is nothing like it. We would not want anyone or anything, even the universe's ways, to come between that bond. We believe we should not bury our children.

And yet, we feel we are the only species that deserve that bond, that privilege, that love.

We take baby chicks away from their mothers' love. It's not a very happy ending for the males, as they are killed immediately for their uselessness on our plates. (Find out what happens to these male chicks. It is pretty sick.) It's also not a very happy life for female chicks, who are immediately taken from their mothers to live tortured lives.

We take baby cows away from their mothers when they are just days old. It is not a pretty scene, this separation. And neither mother nor baby gets a happy ending. I have heard many people say they would never eat veal. They know how horrible baby cows' lives are when they are raised for veal. And they would never support it. Little do they realize that when they drink and eat dairy products, they are supporting the veal industry. The mother cow is kept impregnated throughout her life in order to produce a constant flow of milk. This pregnancy produces many male cows that are used for veal. No, not a happy ending at all.

Baby pigs are also separated from their mothers. She feeds them through caged bars. No cuddling with Mom, no bonding. Shortly after, they are taken away to live their lives behind bars.[39]

Our babies are being killed just as baby animals are being killed. The crime on the streets is out of hand, and our babies are being killed. Others are being taken off to war and killed. Our babies are leaving us way too soon. What goes around comes around.

* * *

Monsanto. Some of you cringed when you read that name. And some of you don't know what Monsanto is. Monsanto is an agrochemical company. They made Agent Orange, a chemical that killed and disfigured over a million people during the Vietnam War era.[40] Monsanto also made PCBs—chemicals that have been proven to cause cancer in animals. Evidence has shown that it also can cause cancer in humans.[41]

Well, as you can see, Monsanto really is a company that will make you cringe. They are a chemical company that seems to only think about making money. They are not concerned with the health and well being of humans in the least. That is what most people who object to Monsanto say. They also say that Monsanto seems to want to take over the world. As the saying goes: he who owns the seed, owns the world. Makes sense—if they own our food, they own us.

Monsanto took a seed. They then injected an insect repellant into the DNA of the cell's seed so that when an insect lands on the plant, it will eat the plant and be killed immediately by the repellant.[42]

This is called genetic modification (GM).[43] The plants that are modified are called genetically modified organisms—GMOs for short.

It might sound like a good thing for our plants to be protected from insects, but on the flip side of things, when they inject the insect repellant into the DNA of our seeds—our food—they change what our food is supposed to be. And studies are showing that this genetically modified food that we are eating is not meant for our bodies. We cannot digest it properly, and studies are showing that it is dangerous to our health.[44] Just Google "Why are GMOs bad?" There is a ton of information about it. Many people are fighting Monsanto. I am grateful for them.

Eighty-eight percent our field corn is genetically modified.[45] Field corn is different than the sweet corn we find in stores. Field corn is used to make tortilla chips, corn flakes, and other foods that contain corn. It's also used to feed animals.[46] We are fed a lot of food that has been genetically modified. And the animals we eat have had their food genetically modified, too.

So, Monsanto is feeding us things that are not really meant for us to eat and that are dangerous to our health.

Karma. That is what is happening in our lives. That is what we do to the animals.

How crazy is it that cows are fed ground up cows? Fish? Chickens? Paper?[47] We grew up believing that cows are herbivores that eat grass. And they are. They are meant to be. But we feed them food that makes them cannibals. They are not meant to eat their own kind, and it is dangerous for their health.

Do you remember the stories about Jeffrey Dahmer, the Milwaukee Cannibal?

Karma.

* * *

What do we want for our children? Don't we want them to have better lives than we had? Don't we always want the best for our children's lives? Yet what do we teach our children? Do we teach them how to have better lives than we have? Do we teach them how to be happy? How can we teach them that if we are not happy ourselves? Some people will say they are happy. And some are. But many people are searching for that happiness in their lives. And right now, they are not happy. Depression rates are pretty high in the United States. Many people are medicating themselves to deaden the pain. Some people don't even realize they are depressed. They just think it is "life."

Happiness. What does it take to be happy? It takes being who you are meant to be. It means following your heart and your passions and loving what you do.

There are so many people I know who choose to stay in a job for the money. Yes, I know that they have families to feed and so they stay in that job to support their families. But some people are living miserable, angry lives. They live their lives with anger, frustration, and bitterness.

I was one of those people. For many years as a teacher, I would leave the building saying to myself, "Damn, you are good." But the last two years of my career, I was an angry, bitter person. I knew I did not belong there anymore, especially when I was told that I could not even say the word "vegan." I was making waves in school, ruffling feathers, being put on the radar. It was time to leave.

Fortunately, I was in service in the New York State retirement system long enough to receive a small pension. With my husband's support, I was able to follow my passion: living a happy life.

But, in general, people don't live happy lives. And we don't teach that to our children. Many of our children are in front of the television or playing video games or on Facebook. They are separated from us not physically, but mentally. They are not even around us long enough for us to teach them.

Karma. What goes around comes around.

We have taken away animals' natural way of being in life and we have told them how they will live. A chicken wants to nest. It wants to teach its babies how to dig. It wants to fly to roost. It wants to do what a chicken does. And a pig wants to roll in the mud and dig his snout in the ground and enjoy the company of his babies and friends. And a cow wants to do what a cow does, and a sheep wants to do what a sheep does. But we don't let them do that. They want to live as they were meant to live. But we don't let them. We separate them from their families and we take away their natural way of being. We confine them and use them as our food, clothing, entertainment, and science experiments. We kill them for our pleasures.

I was a teacher for twenty years. I see what we ask children to do. They are not allowed to be themselves in the classroom. They are told what to do and, by the grades given, they are told that they are not good enough. Some live miserable existences. They just want to be themselves. Some children have a very hard time accepting the status quo. The very difficult ones are the ones who are screaming to be themselves. (An oasis classroom designed to fit a child's natural way of being. Wouldn't that be nice? I know some children who would have flourished in a class designed for them. That is on my list of topics to write about.)

Sean (name changed) was a child I had the good fortune to know for a little while. What a fabulous and interesting child he was! Unfortunately, because of how interesting he was, it was difficult to teach this child the way things had to be taught in a classroom, especially with twenty-five other children. Sean saw things in his own very unique way. He wanted to create a movie. He wanted to draw. He wanted to play. He lived in his own superhero world and did not want to deal with the reality of where he was and what was expected of him.

He wanted fun, creativity, excitement! There was nothing in school for him that he could understand, but he had his own passions. He wore a superhero costume to school one day. Here was Sean to save the day! For five years of his precious life he had to do what he was told to do in school—nothing of which he was interested in doing. Medication was recommended for him. I was so happy his parents said no.

Maybe one day Sean will grow up to save the world. He believes he can. If only we all believed as much as he does.

Many children are in the classrooms just wanting to be themselves. But we don't teach them how to find themselves. That is not the game we play in school. They are told how to live. They are told what to do; they are not encouraged to find what they are meant to be doing in this life. And that does not create happy children or happy societies.

We take away their natural way of being. No wonder we are such an unhappy people.

As we do to the animals, we do to ourselves. Karma.

* * *

Funny how some children are raised with such love while others are abused. We hear these stories all the time in the news: a child locked in a closet for years, a child thrown over the bridge, a child shaken to death, a child beaten to death, a child kidnapped and held hostage for years, and on and on. And we wonder how these things happen. And we feel helpless in being unable to do anything. How could this happen in a civilized society? How could such anger exist? What could drive people to commit such horrible acts? Why did they think it was okay to inflict such pain onto another being?

How come no one helped defend that child, someone who was so helpless and defenseless, who was at the total mercy of his or her caretakers? Why wasn't anyone there to defend that child?

Karma,

Shanti

* * *

This story is new to the second edition. My son persuaded me not to include this topic in the first edition, as he thought it was along the lines of a conspiracy theory. For two years I have been sorry I did not include it. It is about chemtrails. It is not a conspiracy theory. It is my observations. It is my seeing karma.

I love the sky, or at least, I used to love the sky. I used to look up and see the big white, fluffy clouds and see all different kinds of animals. It was a peaceful sight. I loved the sky so much, I told my family to spread my ashes on a mountaintop when I die, so I can be close to the open sky forever.

But the sky troubles me now.

I look up and see planes flying over, leaving trails of smoke that eventually turn into a haze that hides the beautiful blue sky. It was a really cold, snowy winter this year. One day the forecast predicted a beautiful, sunny day. I was excited. I looked forward to the warmth of the sun after this winter. But all I saw as I drove were planes leaving a trail of smoke and turning the sky into a gray haze.

I try not to be an angry person; I really do. But how dare they take my sun away? How dare they think that they will reduce global warming? How dare they spend tax dollars on something so ridiculous? Yes, I do try not to be an angry person, but when I see my sky being clouded up, I get angry. And I wonder if other people look up and feel like I do. Are they too busy to care? Are they too busy driving to their destinations to be concerned? Do they not even see it?

I quickly change my thoughts to forgiving them—for they know not what they do. I know putting anger out in the world does no good.

And then I remember karma, and it makes sense. It does not make me any less angry, but it does make sense.

What do we do to our precious animals on this earth that many call food? Many of our "food" animals never see the light of day. They are housed in their CAFOs—Concentrated Animal Factory Operations—and never see the light. We have taken their light away, and in turn, ours is taken away. Karma.

And then I was thinking: What actually is being sprayed? If they want to help with global warming, why don't they go over deserts where it is really hot and where there are no people? Why are they spraying on top of us? And I think of karma and get even more concerned. What do we do to our teeny creatures of this earth? We spray our food with insecticides, so the creatures die. What are these smoke-filled planes letting fall on us?

Karma. I drive along every day and wonder. I sure do hope there are many more people not just getting disturbed, but acting. If we all speak out, maybe we can do something. Maybe we can stop this craziness before it is too late.

As far as my son and his thinking this is all a conspiracy theory, I am going to send him this link: geoengineeringwatch. org. Close to sixteen million people have visited the site.

Moxie,

Shanti

PS—Moxie means courage. It is what we need.

Are You Ready?

Dear World,

Ask yourself if you are ready. It is not as easy as just saying you are going to do it. It is a commitment. It requires work and doing things just a little bit differently. You saw how the non-cook that I was had to deal with change, but you cooks out there have it easier. You just have to change the ingredients. You don't need to learn the difference between a teaspoon and a tablespoon. You, along with others, can also make it easier for the rest of us.

Chefs, change our restaurants. Make it easy for us to eat. McDonald's, Burger King, and other fast food chains, give the folks who eat your affordable fast food something healthy, something compassionate. (Yes, food can be healthy, compassionate, *and* quick!) Farmers, change your products. Sell us natural, unmodified vegetables. Find a way that's cost-effective for you *and* us. Government, help us do the right thing. Teachers, teach your children well. Parents, feed your children compassionately and healthfully.

They say the definition of insanity is doing the same thing over and over again and expecting different results. Like wishing things were better without doing something different to help the situation.

We all have a choice. We can continue to do things the same old way. We can continue to have a world that is cruel and inhumane and that has a pretty slim chance of survival. *Or* we can start to create a kind and compassionate world.

We have been told repeatedly by the great minds of our world, "Live a life that's compassionate toward all beings."

A misdiagnosis changed my way of thinking, of living, of

being in this world. I had no choice but to be ready. I am grateful to have had that misdiagnosis. It changed my life.

You, on the other hand, will have to decide on your own. Are you ready?

* * *

People are creative, so creative that we can fly through the air, communicate with someone on the other side of the world with the click of a mouse, and enjoy artwork and architecture as beautiful as the *Mona Lisa*, the statue of David, and the Taj Mahal.

If we can create all of that, we can create a better world. We don't have to be cruel. We don't have to live like this.

We can create gardens. We can create ways to feed millions of people while taking care of our earth. We can create people who know not only how to survive, but also thrive on a healthy and compassionate diet. We can create a world that we are proud of, a world that we will be happy to leave to our children. We can do it, if we make our minds up to do it. Some people are already doing amazing work on gardens and in all different ways to create a better world.

It all starts with one person. Watch how the ripple effect works. Watch how the people around you start to change and the people around them start to change and on and on. And pretty soon, you will see that all of us have changed. And if we change ourselves, we change the world. And the children? Tell them we are no longer going to eat animals. They will be happy.

When we hurt someone's spirit, we hurt our own, so it only makes sense that when we help someone's spirit, we also help our own. And when we are kind and compassionate to someone's spirit, we are kind and compassionate to ourselves. So if I am kind and compassionate, that means the world will be kind and compassionate to me? And I just have to change myself, and the world will be at peace? Isn't it pretty awesome to think we have the power to change the world? Just imagine a world of kind and compassionate people.

We often hear, "Be the change you want to see in the world."

Change yourself. We don't have to imagine how to do it anymore. Be kind and compassionate to *all* beings.

Dreaming,

Shanti

So Now What?

Dear World,

I am getting close to finishing this book. It has been an interesting process. The most interesting part is all the people who have shown up in my life just when I needed their help in making this book a reality. It is happening, and I'm excited for the moment when this becomes a published book.

So what happens next—for me, for you, for all of us?

As for me, I will continue to be a vegan activist. I will continue to speak for the animals, for our world, and for peace. I will continue to believe. I have been in Toastmasters for four years. I will continue to learn the skills of speaking in public so that I can get this message out. I am excited for the possibilities. I'm picturing myself selling my books out of the trunk of my car. That sounds like fun to me. I'll see you there!

Yoga and cooking seem to be in my daughter's future. Maybe one day she will have a yoga studio with a small vegan cafe front! Wouldn't that be wonderful! My son will continue to use his computer skills, not only to help his computer-illiterate mother, but also to continue making a peaceful and creative life for himself. My husband will continue to work in the public school system and be an amazing influence on his students. One day he will retire from the school system, but he will continue to follow his passions and use his amazing skills as a master carpenter and landscape artist. And he will continue to do one heck of a job taking care of me! (You can only imagine what it takes for him to do that!)

And what about you? You have a decision to make. Are you one of the "Christine's," who once you know, you have to 'do'? I do hope you will be a "Christine" and—if you will not completely embrace a plant-based lifestyle right away—that you will start eating less meat and start learning how to be vegan.

Or, will you find something in this book to disagree with? Watch *Earthlings* and *Forks Over Knives* if you do disagree. They will make you see.

And if you decide that you *will* do something, what will you do? And how will you do it?

Can you imagine the world in conversation about how to do this? I can.

Can you imagine classrooms all working toward the goal of learning how to change to a vegan lifestyle? I can. What could be more inspiring than working toward peace, health, and a compassionate life? The children would be excited to come to school and learn. And we could actually reverse the fact that this generation is the first generation that will live shorter lives than their parents.[48] People's health could start to improve.

Can you imagine gardens flourishing? Everyone talking and learning about growing and cooking their own compassionate food, and sharing food with others? I can. I can imagine it.

First, imagine. Then, create.

I have listed tips that will help you on this lifestyle path, should you decide to be one of the many people who choose a more conscious, compassionate lifestyle.

Tip # 1 - Share this book and its information with everyone you know. Changing to a vegan lifestyle can be difficult. It is possible to do it alone, but surrounding yourself with a supportive, like-minded community makes things a lot easier. Get your friends and other people you know to do this with you so that you can figure out this new lifestyle together. Share the responsibilities. Make a meal and share it. Take turns with the cooking. Cook or do meal planning together. Anything you can do to make this change less overwhelming.

Suggest the kind of food you want to your local restaurants and supermarkets. Better yet, give them a copy of this book. Know that you have a choice about what you want to spend your money on. Encourage them to feed you right.

I have written this book in a way that is not overwhelming for a person who generally does not read. I have written this for the 90 percent of Americans who can read but don't. I was one of those people. I read when I had to, not to be inspired or entertained. I read when I had to learn about school issues, such as a new math program that I had to learn how to teach. But I wrote this book for all of you with the hope that it will inspire you to learn more, to choose a compassionate lifestyle, to help save our world.

I am also writing to other countries. You have your own issues and statistics. I am more familiar with the United States, and so I speak more to Americans. I know many things are happening where you live also. I hope you are inspired to learn about your part of the world. We are in this together.

Please inspire others to read this, and if your friends can't read, read it to them! Let's get this translated so that all of us can read it.

Yes, I am writing this book to inspire you. Share the inspiration with others. I want to inspire you to make a change in your life for the better, to be a happier person, to make this world a better place, to inspire you to believe that it can be done. Not only is it possible, but it's also important that we lessen the violence that we put out there, both toward the animals and our precious planet. The great teachers of the world have told us so. Let their words inspire you also.

I have met too many people who think my way of thinking will never happen. Why not? Why can't it be done? Margaret Mead said, "Never doubt that a small group of thoughtful, committed citizens can change the world. Indeed, it is the only thing that ever has."[49] There are small groups of committed people all over the world working to make a difference—and they are. The vegan community has been growing in leaps and bounds just in the seven years that I have been vegan. Many people have at least heard the word "vegan."

It is growing fast, thanks to Ellen and Oprah and all the other outspoken TV personalities, the authors and doctors who promote a vegan lifestyle, and all the lesser-known vegans who work behind the scenes planning vegan potlucks, movie showings, and other get-togethers. Many thanks also go to the vegan activists who work tirelessly to get this message out in so many ways, including standing in the street in the middle of winter to hand out vegan pamphlets. There are so many vegans working to inspire you. If you were ready for a reason to change, I hope this book has given you one.

If we all have positive thoughts and gentle actions, our world could be different. Please, world, see what I see. And share it with others.

Tip # 2 - Browse through the supermarket and discover what is available. Hang out in the produce section and learn what kinds of vegetables are available. If you don't know already, learn to tell the difference between cilantro and parsley. I know I still have to look at the labels. The people in the veggie section always seem so willing to answer if you don't know something. However, the best conversation I ever had about veggies was in line at a health food store. The lady in front of us saw that I had two packages of Brussels sprouts. She got so excited when she saw them that she had to run and grab some herself before checking out. Needless to say, the animated conversation between us about how we cook our Brussels sprouts was a scene that got many smiles.

Learn about what kinds of transition foods there are, such as the fake meats and non-dairy cheeses. (Daiya mozzarella for pizza is fabulous!) Your body might be able to handle some of the processed foods. I, on the other hand, still do not react well to processed foods or sugars. My transition has been more toward beans, quinoa, sweet potatoes, and vegetables prepared in many different ways. Seven years ago, I did not know what quinoa was. Today, it is a staple in my house, along with Brussels sprouts, hummus, and baked chickpeas (also called chickpea nuts) with just enough cayenne. I have zucchini patties to prepare today. I love this food! Back in the day, I ate meat because I thought I had to, but I never really liked it. I can honestly say I love my food today. After many meals, it is common for me to exclaim, "That was delicious, absolutely delicious!" You, too, can feel that way after a vegan meal. I promise you.

Tip # 3 - Start browsing the Internet for vegan recipes or buy vegan cookbooks. Discover what the staple ingredients are for your new diet: nutritional yeast flakes, flax seeds, hemp seeds, almond milk, rice milk, and tamari, to name a few. Many of the vegan cookbooks and cooking websites explain how to use these new ingredients. My daughter taught me to read a recipe first. If I like the ingredients separately, then chances are I will like them together in a recipe. And be willing to try new things. My husband probably would not like his macaroni and "cheez" if it did not have the broccoli in it. He just would not admit it!

Tip #4 - Learn to cook. If you are a seasoned chef, then you know how to cook, so get to it! If you are not comfortable in the kitchen, ask someone who knows how to cook to help you, even if it's just enough to get by. Discover the difference between a tablespoon and a teaspoon. Cook with someone or by yourself. Put on some music that keeps you focused, enjoy the experience, and know that you are doing an important thing for all involved. Or, have one person who loves to cook take it on for the whole family, as my daughter has done for mine. But mind you, I know I have to be able to cook when need be, both for my husband and myself. And if you are a young person reading this, bug your parents to let you cook vegan recipes with them. (You have my permission.)

Tip # 5 - Explore vegan resources. At my website, shantiurreta.com, you will find a list of resources that I recommend. I am including books, videos, and websites that will all help you learn more about a vegan diet and lifestyle.

You will also want to learn about health, especially if you are on medication. Make sure you tell a doctor that you are changing your diet; he or she can help you monitor your medications and adjust dosages, as needed.

Learn about the numbers in this book. Someone told me that he was skeptical of large numbers, that fifty-nine billion animals seems to be an exaggeration. Okay, so how about one billion? Is that acceptable? Sigh. If you are skeptical also, Google it. Search how many animals are killed every year.

And then visit a slaughterhouse. Oh, and make sure you are not in certain states where it's illegal.[50] Honestly, I don't think any slaughterhouse would be too open to having you visit. They have a lot to hide. So go on vegan websites. Mercy For Animals and PETA have eye-opening videos that will show you, while keeping you safe.

Tip # 6 - Learn about the plight of the animals (if necessary). I saw this Buddhist saying on Facebook the other day: "Meditate at least twenty minutes every day. If you do not have the time, meditate for an hour." I do not need to keep seeing animal abuse. When I see it in my friends' Facebook posts, it just reminds me why I am doing what I do. But I don't need to see every Mercy For Animals undercover video anymore. I am thoroughly convinced. I am working to stop it.

But seven years ago, I did need to see it. I did not know. I could not have pictured the reality of the situation. I never could have put it into words. Like they say, a picture is worth a thousand words. I could fill this book with a million words, and they would still not be enough to show the horror. If you are not convinced, watch *Earthlings*. It is on YouTube. Most people cannot get through it in one sitting because it is heart-wrenching. But if you still say you are okay eating animal products, it is important to see it. If you don't know what suffering you are sparing yourself the sight of, then you cannot think occasionally of it. You may need to have those images in your head to inspire you to change.

I needed the inspiration to change. I needed the strength to change. I needed the inspiration to fight for the animals. It has not been easy being the person who does not get invited to events because of my diet, because of my passion. Watching the videos gave me the strength that I needed to change, to work for the animals. If people did not want me to go to their events because of it, then I had to say to myself that I had to stay true to my values. I am vegan because of the animals, yes. They drive me. But I'm also vegan for *all* the beings on this planet, both human and nonhuman.

However, I have been to many vegan potlucks. I might not get invited to meat-eating events, but I often get invited to vegan ones and always enjoy the company of like-minded people.

Writing a book on change, on transformation, is not an easy thing to do. Hopefully it will affect the lives of many people. People who have investments in animal agriculture, corporations, and restaurants might not like this idea at first. But I have to believe that they will see this message as more of a positive thing than as a threat to their way of life and to their money. Get this book around. Believe in its message. I believe that we can lay down the guns and knives, and all work for peace. And we can stop the horrible massacre of billions of animals.

I had to have strength. I had to watch those videos. If you can still say that you won't go vegan, watch the videos and then say that. Or, if you have decided to go vegan but need encouragement, watch the videos.

If you need strength to change, watch them. If you know that you will change just because you know it is the right thing to do, then you may not need to watch them. As the Buddhist saying goes, "Twenty minutes or an hour." Please watch them, especially *Earthlings*, and then decide what you are willing to have on your plate.

Tip # 7 - Follow your heart. If you feel right now that all you want to do is change for yourself, for your health, then do so. The animals will benefit. If you feel compelled to work for the animals, or the planet, or the people on our earth, then do so. Follow your heart. It will tell you the right thing to do. No matter how difficult the challenge may seem at first, follow your heart. It will give you the strength.

Tip # 8 - Talk to vegans. Learn from them. Listen to what they have to say. We actually are pretty nice people, in spite of what some of you may have heard about our "pushiness." Please excuse us. We "push" because we are passionate about stopping the terror.

Tip # 9 - Be happy! Last but not least, *be happy for yourself* for accepting the gifts of health, consciousness, and peace. I share them with you.

Lovingly,

Shanti

Food Ideas

Dear World,

I am including some food ideas and recipes here. They are the ones that have become favorites in my family's quest to live on a plant-based diet.

Quick meal ideas (heat-and-eat style):

- Gardein turk'y cutlets are my husband's favorite. Put the cutlet in a sandwich with some mustard, heat the included sauce packet for some mashed potatoes, and add some greens (kale, broccoli, spinach—whatever calls to you)
- Amy's non-dairy bean burritos
- Fake meat sandwich slices with vegan cheese and Vegenaise (vegan mayonnaise) on toast

Quick meal ideas with little prep:

- Fakin' Bacon on a Daiya grilled cheese sandwich with tomato
- Scrambled tofu made like scrambled eggs (more delicious than you would think)
- Salads, steamed broccoli, or kale with sea salt and fresh lemon juice, and other greens or veggies make great sides. Add a glob of hummus or some avocado, and then you're really set!

* * *

I know some of you were wishing you had the recipes in this book that I mentioned, so I typed some up for you (thanks to my wonderful daughter). Choose one at a time. Gather the ingredients for just one and give it a try. And then try another recipe. You will be surprised how easy this change can be if you don't give up.

Roasted Chickpeas
(Slightly adapted from Myra Kornfeld)[51]

You will be addicted to these chickpeas after you perfect them for your personal tastes. It took me quite a few tries experimenting with the spices and baking time to make it just the way I like. Feel free to experiment with yours, and make sure you toss them often.

Ingredients
2 (15-ounce) cans chickpeas, drained and rinsed,
    or 3 cups freshly cooked chickpeas
1 tablespoon plus 1 teaspoon extra virgin olive oil
2½ tablespoons fresh lemon juice
1 teaspoon sea salt
2 pinches cayenne pepper (be careful; this is hot!)

Directions
1. Preheat oven to 415 degrees Fahrenheit. Drain the chickpeas in a colander for as long as your patience will allow—the drier the beans are, the better. Pat dry with a paper towel or clean dishtowel.
2. In a mixing bowl, combine the chickpeas, lemon juice, olive oil, sea salt, and cayenne. Mix with a spatula until evenly coated.
3. Pour the beans into a shallow baking pan. (The pan is the right size if all beans fit in a single layer. The pan is too big if there is more than ¼ inch between each bean, and too small if they are snug like sardines.)

4. Bake for approximately 30 to 35 minutes. Toss after 10 minutes, then every 6 minutes until cooked. Because the exact time will vary based on your oven and altitude, use the 35-minute cooking time as a guideline. What you really want is a dark golden color to the chickpeas and a crunchy texture without being overly dry. When the beans start to take on a light golden color, be vigilant about watching the oven. Open the door every couple minutes to check the color and taste one to test the crunchiness.

* * *

Veggie Mac 'n' Cheez

Ingredients
3½ cups pasta (elbow or rotini)
3½ cups boiling water
½ cup soy margarine (such as Earth Balance)
½ cup spelt flour (all-purpose would also work)
1½ teaspoons sea salt
2 tablespoons soy sauce or tamari sauce
1½ teaspoons garlic powder
Pinch turmeric
¼ cup extra virgin olive oil
1 cup nutritional yeast flakes
   (available at most health food stores and online)
1 cup broccoli florets, chopped into bite-size pieces
   (can use blanched or frozen that has been thawed)
Pinch paprika

Directions
1. Preheat the oven to 350 degrees Fahrenheit and set aside a 13 x 9-inch glass casserole dish.
2. Cook the pasta according to package directions. Strain the pasta and run under cool water to stop the cooking process. Drain.
3. Bring the 3½ cups of water to a boil.
4. In a large saucepan, melt the margarine over medium-low heat. Whisk in the flour and continue whisking until the mixture is smooth and begins to bubble.
5. Stir in the boiling water, salt, soy sauce or tamari, garlic powder, and turmeric. Whisk until all ingredients are dissolved.
6. Continue cooking until the sauce thickens and bubbles. Whisk in the olive oil and nutritional yeast flakes.
7. Mix ¾ of the sauce with the pasta, then add the broccoli

florets. Pour the mixture into the casserole dish. Pour the remaining sauce over the top of the pasta and sprinkle with paprika.

8. Bake for 25 minutes, then broil for 2 minutes to lightly brown the top of the cheez.

* * *

Stuffed Pasta Shells

Ingredients
2 dozen jumbo pasta shells
2 teaspoons extra virgin olive oil
3 cups drained extra firm tofu
2 cups Soy Cream (recipe follows) ·
2 tablespoons onion powder
2 tablespoons dried basil
2 tablespoons dried oregano
1 tablespoon garlic powder
2 teaspoons sea salt
1 cup frozen spinach, thawed and chopped
5 cups pasta sauce (fresh or jarred)

Directions
1. Preheat the oven to 350 degrees Fahrenheit and set aside a 13 x 9-inch casserole dish.
2. Cook the pasta shells very al dente. Rinse under cool water, then toss with olive oil. Set aside.
3. Drain the tofu. Place small chunks in fine cheesecloth and lightly squeeze out excess water. If you don't have cheesecloth, you can use your hands to squeeze the tofu. I also have found using a reusable nut-milk bag works the best. (Nut-milk bags are available in health food stores and online.)
4. Prepare the soy cream. In a large bowl, combine the drained tofu, soy cream, onion powder, basil, oregano, garlic powder, salt, and spinach.
5. Line the bottom of the casserole dish with a thin layer of pasta sauce.
6. Fill the pasta shells with the tofu mixture and place in the casserole dish. Cover the shells with the remaining pasta sauce.

7. Cover with aluminum foil and bake for 45 minutes. Remove the foil and bake for an additional 10 minutes.

Soy Cream (for Stuffed Pasta Shells)

Ingredients
1 cup unsweetened soymilk
½ teaspoon sea salt
½ teaspoon onion powder
1 cup extra virgin olive oil
2 tablespoons fresh lemon juice

Directions
1. Combine the soymilk, salt, and onion powder in a blender and blend on high for 10 seconds.
2. Slowly add the oil while the blender is on high. Blend for a full minute after all the oil has been added.
3. Stop the blender, add the lemon juice, and blend on high for 10 seconds. The mixture should thicken to a mayonnaise-like consistency.

* * *

Raw Chocolate Bites
(Slightly adapted from thisrawsomeveganlife.com)[52]

Ingredients
2 cups walnuts
1½ cups chopped dates
½ cup unsweetened coconut flakes
⅓ cup cocoa or cacao powder
¼ cup hemp seeds
3 tablespoons melted coconut oil,
    plus more as needed to bind ingredients
2 tablespoons ground flaxseeds
¼ teaspoon vanilla extract
¼ teaspoon sea salt
Pinch cinnamon

Directions
1. Blend all ingredients in a food processor until well combined. Pinch a section of the chocolate; if it crumbles, add more coconut oil until the chocolate stays firm.
2. Spread into an 8 x 8-inch casserole dish, cover with plastic wrap or the dish's lid, and refrigerate until solid.
3. Cut into squares or use cookie cutters for shapes.

* * *

Balsamic Mixed Bean Salad

Ingredients
3 cups mixed beans (pink, kidney, chickpeas) or salad
   beans (canned or fresh)
1 cup green beans (fresh or frozen)
¼ cup chopped red onion
3 tablespoons balsamic vinegar
2 tablespoons extra virgin olive oil
2 tablespoons chopped fresh parsley
¾ teaspoon chili powder
½ teaspoon garlic powder
½ teaspoon sea salt
Pinch black pepper

Directions
1. Empty beans into a colander, rinse, and set aside to drain.
2. Put a handful of ice into a large bowl and fill with water. Set aside.
3. Bring a pot of water to boil and have a slotted spoon ready on the side. You will be blanching the green beans. This means you will be cooking the green beans briefly, then placing them in ice water. This stops the cooking process so that they don't get mushy like they would if they were left to cool on their own.
4. If using fresh green beans, cut them into 1-inch pieces. Place half of the beans in the boiling water and cook for 20 to 25 seconds until they turn bright green. Remove the beans from the water with the slotted spoon and submerge them in the ice water for 30 seconds. Remove from the ice water and drain in a colander. Repeat with the second batch.
5. If using frozen green beans, use the same blanching and draining process as with fresh green beans but only boil

for approximately 10 seconds. Any longer and the beans might become too soft.

6. Place the beans, green beans, and the red onion, olive oil, parsley, chili powder, garlic powder, salt, and pepper in a large bowl. Mix well to incorporate, and chill in the refrigerator for at least an hour before serving.

* * *

Caramelized Brussels Sprouts

Ingredients

8 ounces Brussels sprouts

2 tablespoons extra virgin olive oil

¼ teaspoon plus pinch sea salt, divided

Juice from ½ a lemon

Directions

1. Peel off the outer leaves of the sprouts. Instead of washing the sprouts, use a dry paper towel to brush off any dirt.
2. Cut the sprouts in half lengthwise, so that each piece has half of the root portion. Cut larger sprouts in quarters so that the pieces are similar in size and will cook evenly.
3. Heat the olive oil in a sauté pan over medium heat. The pan is ready when a sprout dropped into the oil makes a sizzling sound.
4. Add sprouts and ¼ teaspoon of the sea salt to the pan. Toss to combine. Using tongs, place each sprout flat-side down.
5. Turn down the heat to medium-low and sauté, uncovered, for approximately 7 minutes. Occasionally, shake the pan back and forth to prevent sticking. Avoid over-stirring, as it will cause the sprouts to fall apart.
6. After the 7 minutes, flip the sprouts to the rounded side and cook for 3 minutes.
7. Flip the sprouts again so that the flat side is down and cook for another 4 minutes. Remove from the heat and add remaining pinch of sea salt and a generous squeeze of lemon juice.

* * *

Bean Dip
This is a hit at parties!

Ingredients
2 cans vegetarian refried beans
Tofu-Cilantro Sour Cream (recipe follows)
½ cup black olives
¼ cup scallions, white and green parts, thinly sliced
1 cup chopped tomato
Tortilla chips or cut veggies, for dipping

Directions
1. Layer the refried beans on the bottom of a 9-inch pie dish.
2. Layer the Tofu-Cilantro Sour Cream over the refried beans.
3. Top with black olives, scallions, and tomatoes.

* * *

Tofu-Cilantro Sour Cream
Makes a delicious garnish for soups and can also be used as a dip or as a topping for baked potatoes and Mexican dishes. Makes 3 cups.

Ingredients
2 teaspoons agar-agar powder (available in health
  food stores and online)
4 tablespoons fresh lemon juice
2 tablespoons fresh lime juice
16 ounces firm tofu
1/3 cup extra virgin olive oil
¼ cup chopped cilantro
2 tablespoons safflower oil
1½ teaspoons salt
½ teaspoon minced garlic
Pinch cayenne

Directions
1. In a nonreactive bowl, dissolve the agar-agar in the lemon and lime juices.
2. Blanch the tofu for 5 minutes, drain, and allow to cool for 20 minutes. Crumble the tofu and transfer to a blender. Blend until smooth. (You can also use a food processor for this.)
3. Add the olive oil, cilantro, safflower oil, salt, garlic, and cayenne and blend until smooth and well incorporated. Covered sour cream will keep in the refrigerator for up to 3 days.

* * *

Not-Tuna Salad
Enjoy as a sandwich, on crackers, or as a side dish!

Ingredients
1½ cups cooked or canned chickpeas (garbanzo beans), drained and rinsed
¼ cup celery, finely chopped
¼ cup shallots, finely chopped
3 to 4 tablespoons Vegenaise (or any dairy-free mayonnaise)
1 tablespoon nutritional yeast flakes
1 tablespoon fresh lemon juice
1 teaspoon kelp flakes
½ teaspoon sea salt
⅓ teaspoon paprika
Pinch fresh black pepper

Directions
1. In a food processor, pulse chickpeas 2 to 3 times until crumbled. Do not over-process to the point where the beans become a paste. Pulse just until they are cut into smaller pieces, then transfer to a large bowl.
2. Add the celery, shallots, Vegenaise, nutritional yeast, lemon juice, kelp flakes, salt, paprika, and pepper to the chickpeas, and stir to combine.

I hope you enjoy!

Shanti

Epilogue

Dear World,

I am seven months into writing this book and am working as fast as I can. It has been interesting getting advice from others on how to even begin a book, working with writers' workshop groups, and talking to people about what I am doing. People really seem to like the idea of this book when I speak to them, as long as I don't give them too much or too little information. It seems as though you have to read the whole book or nothing at all.

In my editing process, I have asked people I know or happen to meet to read my draft and give me their opinions so that I can improve my work. The comments have been mixed critiques. My vegan friends give me two thumbs up and say that I have it all there. They are happy that this book will be out in the world.

Some people whom I have asked to read it have chosen not to get back to me. Not really sure why. I know they have read it. Does it take some time to let it sink in? Do they just not know how to respond? I am not really sure.

And then there are those who have responded. One person told me that they just don't agree with karma. They don't understand it. Of all the reasons I give in this book to embrace a vegan lifestyle, I wonder why that one is so important to them. What about the suffering, the horrendous killing, the planetary issues, the health issues, the quotes from the great minds of the world? Why just pick one thing in this book to disagree with? I don't understand their thought processes, but hopefully other people who choose to use the idea of karma as a reason *not* to change will find another reason in this book to be inspired to make a change.

I have also have received the exact opposite reaction. I met Bruce, a seventy-year-old man, while searching for my husband in

Home Depot. Bruce was there handing out home repair estimate papers. We engaged in a conversation about animals. He noticed I was wearing a sweatshirt promoting the animal welfare organization In Defense of Animals. (This time, I dodged the smirks from my husband about wearing vegan messages on my clothes!) Bruce spent the next ten minutes telling me about his rescued dogs. It was quite obvious this man loved his dogs. One conversation led to the next, and he offered to read my book. Bruce, I am happy to say, gave up animal products as soon as he read this book. Bruce went on a vegan diet and became one of my best friends. I am so very, very grateful.

* * *

Life has a way of taking us down the road we were meant to be on. I have to take a little break from sitting here and editing.

My nephew was taken from us this week in a tragic car accident. He was a beautiful twenty-five-year-old boy who was just starting a well-paying job and a new life in Michigan with his girlfriend. And I think of societal karma, and I cry. Here is a baby who was taken from our graces.

He was a special friend to my son—they were more friends than cousins. They both shared a love of computers. They both shared deep conversations about life and death. Now there is a void in my son's heart. And a void in mine and in the rest of our family's.

I have never had anyone so young taken from my family before. The universe took away a loved one of mine—a baby—before his time.

Karma. We do that to the animals. We take away their loved ones before their time. I feel their pain. Why do we think that we are the only ones who are capable of feeling emotional pain? Mother cows bellow mercilessly when their babies are taken away. Pigs scream. Chickens, I don't know. But I do know how it feels to have a baby taken away. Animals feel, too. And what gives us the right to *cause* their pain? What gives us the right to ignore the fact that they do actually feel pain? What gives us the right to ignore the fact that we cause it?

The animals that we eat—after slaughtering them—die early in life, much earlier than they would have if they had been able to live out their natural lives.

I am not too fond of societal karma right now. Quite possibly, it took away our baby.

***

And so now I must end my letters with a few final thoughts:

It has been my pleasure speaking with you. I wish you luck. I do hope we meet up again.

I sincerely hope, pray, and dream that you are a "Christine," and that once you know, you must do—because now you know, now you see.

With much love until we meet again,

Shanti

> *"Unless someone like you cares a whole awful lot, nothing is going to get better. It's not."*
> —Dr. Seuss (from *The Lorax*)[53]

Thank You

This book was written in the span of about eight months. In that time, some people have come and gone in my life. Some people are my occasional contacts—acquaintances on some level. And others are constants in my life. I am truly grateful to all of you who have helped me make this book a reality. You all made an impact on my life in some way or another. I live in gratitude.

I am truly grateful for believing and living the concept of being in awe of the power to manifest. I believed in this book. I am grateful to those who believed in this book with me.

Thank you to all those whom I have quoted for allowing me to use these words. Thank you so much for being models for compassion and peace.

Thank you to Dr. Brightman, who was wise enough to steer me on this path.

Thank you to Dr. Will Tuttle, author of *The World Peace Diet*, for being one of my greatest teachers.

Thank you to John Robbins, author of *Diet for a New America*, for showing me the beautiful side of animals.

Thank you to Joaquin Phoenix, narrator of the *Earthlings* documentary, for embedding unforgettable pictures in my head that will always be the driving force for what I do.

Thank you to all vegans who walk this path with me. I am grateful for your company. I am happy that you have a compelling book to share with your friends. I know these are your words also.

Thank you to Christine for being my friend. Thank you for being open to knowing and for "doing" once you knew.

Thank you to Mr. Calabro's and Mr. Lepore's classes. You inspired me to write this book so you, too, could read it.

Thank you to Dr. Anthony Gantt, author and public speaker, for telling me I had to write a book.

Thank you to Mary for being that person who made sure I went "to glow."

Thank you to Angel for always provoking me and helping me "to speak in the real world."

Thank you to my Toastmasters group for supporting me in getting this message out and in helping me to find my voice.

Thank you to the Somers and Mahopac Writers' Workshops for your ears and words.

Thank you to "Home Depot" Bruce for seeing, for getting it, for making the changes in your life, and for believing in this book.

Thank you to Kaitlin for being such a talented editor *and* for becoming vegan in your research for this book.

Thank you to Aimee, my second editor. I edited your work in first grade. You have grown and now are editing my work.

Thank you to Casey and his staff from Vegan Publishers. I am grateful you read my book and believed in it enough to publish a second edition.

Thank you to C.J., my son, for always being my toughest critic and for all of your computer assistance. I could not have done this without you!

Thank you to Janani, my daughter, for all the food that nourished me while I worked. And thanks for your wonderful research skills and recipe help.

Thank you to my husband for loving me. I am grateful I had *you* to live this story with.

Thank you to John Lennon for inspiring me to "Imagine."

Thank you to Albert Schweitzer for being my guide.

Thank you to those who have crossed my path at some moment or another. Each and every one of you has made an impact on my life, and for that, I am grateful.

Love always,

Shanti

Notes

1. James Brabazon, "Sermon, February 23, 1919," *Albert Schweitzer: Essential Writings* (Maryknoll, NY: Orbis Books, 2005), 143.
2. 2. Charles Stahler, "How Often Do Americans Eat Vegetarian Meals? And How Many Adults in the U.S. Are Vegan?," *Vegetarian Journal* 30, no. 4 (2011): 10.
3. Albert Schweitzer, *The Philosophy of Civilization* (Amherst, NY: Prometheus Books, 1987), 344.
4. Joel Fuhrman, quoted on cover of Mike Anderson, *Eating*, 3rd ed. (2008), DVD.
5. Winston J. Craig and Ann Reed Mangels, "Position of the American Dietetic Association: Vegetarian Diets," *Journal of the American Dietetic Association* 109, no. 7 (July 2009): 1266.
6. Schweitzer, *The Philosophy of Civilization*, 344.
7. T. Colin Campbell and Thomas M. Campbell II, *The China Study: The Most Comprehensive Study of Nutrition Ever Conducted and the Startling Implications for Diet, Weight Loss and Long-term Health* (Dallas: BenBella Books, 2005), 56.
8. Stahler, "How Often Do Americans Eat Vegetarian Meals?," 10.
9. Gary Smith, The Thinking Vegan Facebook page, accessed March 5, 2015, http://www.facebook.com/thethinkingvegan.
10. Whitney Metz, "Guilt," *Hello Poetry*, February 2, 2010, http://hellopoetry.com/poem/guilt-1/.
11. Will Tuttle, *The World Peace Diet: Eating for Spiritual Health and Social Harmony* (New York: Lantern Books, 2005), 11.
12. PETA, *Glass Walls* (Norfolk, VA: PETA, 2010), DVD.
13. James Brabazon, *Albert Schweitzer: A Biography* (Syracuse, NY: Syracuse University Press, 2000), 243–263.
14. Boris Worm et al., "Impacts of Biodiversity Loss on Ocean Ecosystem Services," *Science* 314, no. 5800 (November 3, 2006), doi:10.1126/science.1132294., 790.
15. Richard H. Schwartz, "The Case Against Eating Fish," *North American Vegetarian Society*, accessed July 10, 2013, http://www.navs-online.org/animal_issues/fish_fishing/troubledwaters.php.
16. "Livestock a Major Threat to Environment," *FAO Newsroom*, November 29, 2006, http://www.fao.org/newsroom/en/news/2006/1000448/index.html.
17. "59 Billion Land and Sea Animals Killed for Food in the US in 2009," *Free From Harm*, January 15, 2011, http://freefromharm.org/farm-animal-welfare/59-billion-land-and-sea-animals-killed-for-food-in-the-us-in-2009/.
18. David M. Schwartz, *How Much Is a Million?* 20th anniversary reissue ed. (New York: HarperCollins, 2004).
19. Livestock a Major Threat to Environment."
20. Greenpeace Tumblr page, accessed February 7, 2015, http://greenpeaceusa.tumblr.com/post/93508666790/the-earth-is-4-6-billion-years-old-scaling-to-46.
21. "Meat Production Wastes Natural Resources," *PETA*, accessed July 12, 2013, http://www.peta.org/issues/Animals-Used-For-Food/Meat-Wastes-Natural-Resources.aspx.
22. John Robbins, *Diet for a New America* (Tiburon, CA: H J Kramer, 1998), ch.12, 328.
23. Ginny Messina, "Recommended Supplements for Vegans," *The Vegan R.D.* (blog), November 28, 2010, http://www.theveganrd.com/2010/11/recommended-supplements-for-vegans.html.
24. "Meat Production Wastes Natural Resources," PETA.
25. Sandra Postel, "Texas Water District Acts to Slow Depletion of the Ogallala Aquifer," *National Geographic*, February 7, 2012, http://newswatch.nationalgeographic.com/2012/02/07/texas-water-district-acts-to-slow-depletion-of-the-ogallala-aquifer/.

26. Hope Bohanec, "California's Drought—Who's Really Using all the Water?" *One Green Planet*, January 24, 2014. http://www.onegreenplanet.org/news/californias-drought-whos-really-using-all-the-water/.

27. "Facts about Pollution from Livestock Farms," *Natural Resources Defense Council*, last modified February 21, 2013, http://www.nrdc.org/water/pollution/ffarms.asp.

28. Food and Agricultural Organization of the United Nations, *Livestock's Long Shadow: Environmental Issues and Options* (Rome: FAO, 2006): 272.

29. Peter Della Santina, "Karma," in *The Tree of Enlightenment: An Introduction to the Major Traditions of Buddhism* (Chico Dharma Study Foundation, 1997), 95–105, http://www.buddhanet.net/pdf_file/tree-enlightenment.pdf.

30. Mahatma Gandhi, quoted in "Can the Greatness of a Nation…," *PETA*, accessed July 19, 2013, http://www.peta.org/features/gandhi.aspx.

31. Philip Wollen, interview by Gary Smith, "The Thinking Vegan Interview with Philip Wollen," *The Thinking Vegan* (blog), July 31, 2012, http://thethinkingvegan.com/interviews/the-thinking-vegan-interview-with-philip-wollen/.

32. Brian Morton, "Falser Words Were Never Spoken," *The New York Times*, August 29, 2011, http://www.nytimes.com/2011/08/30/opinion/falser-words-were-never-spoken.html.

33. C. David Coats, *Old MacDonald's Factory Farm: The Myth of the Traditional Farm and the Shocking Truth about Animal Suffering in Today's Agribusiness* (New York: Continuum, 1991), 13.

34. American Society for the Prevention of Cruelty to Animals, *A Growing Problem: Selective Breeding in the Chicken Industry* (New York: ASPCA, 2014), 3.

35. Neal D. Barnard, "Breaking the Food Seduction," *Physicians Committee for Responsible Medicine*, accessed July 15, 2013, http://www.pcrm.org/search/?cid=1290.

36. "The Egg Industry," *PETA*, accessed July 15, 2013, http://www.peta.org/issues/Animals-Used-For-Food/Egg-Industry.aspx.

37. "The Pork Industry," *PETA*, accessed July 15, 2013, http://www.peta.org/issues/Animals-Used-For-Food/Pork-Industry.aspx.

38. "The Dairy Industry," *PETA*, accessed July 15, 2013, http://www.peta.org/issues/Animals-Used-For-Food/Dairy-Industry.aspx.

39. "Life of a Pig on a Factory Farm," *MSPCA*, accessed February 7, 2015, http://www.mspca.org/programs/animal-protection-legislation/animal-welfare/farm-animal-welfare/factory-farming/pigs/pigs-on-a-factory-farm.html.

40. "Agent Orange," *History*, accessed February 7, 2015, http://www.history.com/topics/vietnam-war/agent-orange.

41. Food & Water Watch, *Monsanto: A Corporate Profile* (Washington, DC: Food & Water Watch, 2013), 4.

42. Ibid.

43. "The GE Process," *Institute for Responsible Technology*, accessed July 16, 2013, http://www.responsibletechnology.org/gmo-basics/the-ge-process.

44. "Health Risks," *Institute for Responsible Technology*, accessed July 16, 2013, http://www.responsibletechnology.org/health-risks.

45. "FAQs on GMOs," *Whole Foods Market*, accessed February 22, 2015, http://www.wholefoodsmarket.com/faqs-gmos.

46. "The Difference Between Sweet Corn and Field Corn," *Agricultured*, accessed February 22, 2015, http://www.agricultured.org/difference-between-sweet-corn-and-field-corn/.

47. "They Eat What? The Reality of Feed at Animal Factories," *Union of Concerned Scientists*, last modified August 8, 2006, http://www.ucsusa.org/food_and_agriculture/our-failing-food-system/industrial-agriculture/they-eat-what-the-reality-of.html.

48. "Overweight in Children," *American Heart Association*, last modified on January 10,

2013, http://www.heart.org/HEARTORG/GettingHealthy/Overweight-in-Children_UCM_304054_Article.jsp.

49. Nancy Lutkehaus, *Margaret Mead: The Making of an American Icon* (Princeton, NJ: Princeton University Press, 2008), 4.

50. Mark Morford, "Something Like Meat But Not Meat," *The Huffington Post*, June 11, 2014, http://www.huffingtonpost.com/mark-morford/something-like-meat-but-n_b_5482878.html.

51. Myra Kornfeld, *The Voluptuous Vegan: More Than 200 Sinfully Delicious Recipes for Meatless, Eggless, and Dairy-Free Meals* (New York: Clarkson Potter, 2000), 121.

52. Emily von Euw, *This Rawsome Vegan Life* (blog), accessed March 21, 2015, http://www.thisrawsomeveganlife.com/.

53. Dr. Seuss, *The Lorax* (New York: Random House, 1971).